No Limits

*By Harry C. Cordellos
and Janet Wells*

Guru's

Feeding a civilization.

First published in the United States of America in 1993. This second edition revised and re-issued in 2001 by Guru's Press, 428 E. Winchester Avenue, Suite 240, Salt Lake City, UT 84107, www.gurusfoundation.com. Book design by Kenneth Turbeville. Cover designed by Rick Bennett.

10 9 8 7 6 5 4 3 2

Library of Congress Card Number: 00-110107
Cordellos, Harry & Wells, Janet, 2001
  No Limits
  2nd Edition

ISBN 0-97010-26-3-1

DEDICATION:
On the 50th anniversary of its world famous water ski shows, this book is dedicated to the Cypress Gardens ski team and staff, who truly know the meaning of "no limits." Thank you for all your encouragement and enthusiastic support through the years and for including me so often in your programs. May your shows continue to entertain Cypress Gardens guests for at least another fifty years.

YOUR FRIEND
HARRY

When we can accept ourselves as we are and not be concerned about those things we lack, and when we can face each new challenge with faith, determination and confidence, nothing is impossible.

HARRY CORDELLOS

ACKNOWLEDGMENTS

Harry Cordellos: I'm grateful to the many partners who have guided me, to the teachers and friends who have encouraged me along the way, and to my family for their support (even if they didn't always understand my goals!). Thanks also to Janet Wells and Dr. Wayman Spence, for their time and energy in making *No Limits* a reality.

Janet Wells: Kudos and thanks to Harry for his infallible memory and indomitable attitude; Dr. Wayman Spence for bringing impossible dream stories to life; Terri Johnson and Margaret Leary for judicious editing; Paul Frassetto and Kate Degnan for epicurean support and technical advice; Bob Condon for bottomless friendship; my parents, Alison and Ed Wells, for getting me out of diapers and onto the trail; and especially to Mark Ripperda, for love, support, encouragement— and a secure belay.

FOREWORD

In 1992, along with eight others, Harry Cordellos and I received the U.S. Junior Chamber of Commerce Healthy American Fitness Leaders Award. I was thrilled to share this award ceremony with Harry.

I first met Harry in 1970 when I spoke at a medical meeting in San Francisco. Since then, we've become close friends, personally and professionally. Harry comes to the Cooper Clinic in Dallas every year to be examined on our treadmill as part of our ongoing cardiovascular research. His fitness level has stayed remarkably high since 1975 when he was first tested, and at age 53 he still performs better than almost all 25-year-olds we examine.

Harry is a pioneer—one who has gone before to make way for others to follow. He is recognized as one of the first totally blind athletes to run marathons, compete in alpine and Nordic skiing, water-ski at Cypress Gardens as a performer, and even run steeplechases. As a result of Harry's participation, the Boston Marathon has added categories for the blind and disabled. Because so many disabled individuals have heard Harry speak, they too have begun to participate in sports.

Leadership is a trademark for all great Americans, certainly for Harry. He has talked, persuaded, inspired, and motivated so many thousands of people that his name and feats are known throughout the country. He has helped organize sporting events, served as official consultant to a myriad of sporting and athletic activities, and has made innumerable suggestions that have been adopted by national organizations for the disabled. There is no more respected voice and acknowledged leader for disabled athletes than Harry Cordellos.

Teaching people not to quit, not to give in to their disabilities, but to live happier, healthier, and more productive lives by conquering their limitations and fears and recognizing their potential—that is the message of Harry Cordellos. Listening to him, watching him, knowing what he has accomplished in spite of his blindness, I am amazed and inspired. You too will be amazed and inspired by Harry's story, a very convincing testament to the fact that we have no limits.

—Dr. Kenneth Cooper
Author and Director of the Cooper Aerobics Center, Dallas

FRONTISPIECE

"So much has been given to me; I have no time to ponder over that which has been denied." **—Helen Keller**

"Whatever you can do or dream you can, begin it. Boldness has genius, power, and magic in it." **—Goethe**

Chapter 1

THROUGH THE FOG

"There shouldn't be any limitations on the blind when it comes to keeping fit. There are all kinds of things they can do. But some people are afraid, and there's no accessibility, no one to run or swim with. It's very easy to make excuses. Harry's one of my classic examples of people who think they have excuses, then overcome them."
–Dr. Kenneth H. Cooper
Author and Director, Cooper Aerobics Center, Dallas.

One overcast summer day, 17-year-old Harry Cordellos took the family dog for an afternoon walk along San Francisco's Ocean Beach. The pair stopped at an empty warehouse parking lot across the street from the beach boardwalk, where Rickey, a large friendly Collie, dropped the piece of driftwood from his mouth and waited, barking and wagging his tail.

"It was time for our favorite game," Harry remembers. "I picked up the stick and threw it as far as I could towards the other end of the parking lot. As he took off to fetch it, I would run as fast as I could in the opposite direction and hide behind the warehouse."

Typical behavior for a boy and his dog—except that Harry, eyes severely damaged by glaucoma, could see little more than light and shadow and blurs of color.

"It didn't bother me to run when my eyes weren't clear. I thought the parking lot was empty. I was running at top speed when, Wham! Something seemed to leap in front of me and stopped me with a tremendous jolt. I fell back on the ground and heard a loud crash and the sound of glass shattering around me. I had been knocked off my feet, my head was throbbing and I felt dizzy.

"I didn't know what had happened—I thought a car might have crashed nearby. I sat for a minute, trying to catch my breath and see if anything was broken. I figured it was just another one of my near misses, so I crawled on my hands and knees until I found my glasses a few feet away, bent but not broken. Then, there, right in front of me was one of the metal light poles in the parking lot. I realized I had run smack into it, hard enough to knock the heavy glass reflector at the top at least 15 feet to the ground.

"I hadn't seen that pole at all. When I thought of what would have happened if that bulb had hit me instead of the dirt, I vowed never, ever to run again."

That was in 1955. A few years later, on a lake in the foothills of California's Sierra Nevada mountains, with a pair of water skis, a rope and two words, "Hit it!", Harry's life changed forever. Now, not only does he run, but he does it with speed and stamina, holding national titles in just about every track and field event in his age group. He has run more than 42,000 miles, competing in marathons all over the country. And he completed America's premier ultra-athletic event—the Ironman Triathlon in Hawaii. He is a world-class blind water-skier, winning medals in trick skiing events and jumping competitions. He also snow skiis, bowls, bicycles, golfs, swims, dives, kayaks, windsurfs, and builds intricate wood crafts. His accomplishments seem endless. And he's always ready to leap at a new challenge. No wonder he's been dubbed "The World's Greatest Blind Athlete." It's a moniker that embarrasses Harry, but as an individual who has been an inspiration and source of amazement to many, it's a phrase that follows him everywhere. As sports health expert Dr. Kenneth Cooper likes to say, "For Harry, blindness is not so much a handicap as it is an inconvenience."

Harry never dared imagine himself growing up to be a superachieving athlete. It seemed inconceivable, even for the far-flung dreams of childhood: He had enough competition battling the glaucoma that slowly robbed him of his vision. His eyes might be clear in the morning; then, by afternoon, "the fog," as he called it, would descend. Hazy rainbows of light would dance in front of his eyes, turning the world into a confusing, disorienting blur.

By the time he was 20 years old, he had to face total irreparable blindness. Such a loss could be overwhelming, but Harry learned to do more than simply cope and adapt. He began to push the envelope of what was possible for someone without sight.

Harry's life is about breaking free from limitations. His story is one of overcoming seemingly insurmountable obstacles and seeking out challenges. It's about partnership, faith and trust in God. But his life also is about facing fears and failure, and that is the lifespring of his strength and achievement: Harry allows himself to fall down or to make mistakes, then he simply gets back up, dusts himself off and gets back into the game.

Harry Cordellos faced daunting physical odds from the day he came into the world. Born November 28, 1937, totally blind from glaucoma, he soon developed a heart murmur from a bout with scarlet fever. Glaucoma, one of the leading causes of blindness in the United States, is a disease that interferes with the clear, transparent liquid that flows continuously through the inner eye. When the eye's drainage system is blocked, the fluid pressure inside the eye skyrockets and can damage the optic nerve.

The drainage system for Harry's eyes was totally defective when he was born; he had eight operations before he was a year old, and these initially helped relieve the pressure buildup in his eyes. His sight was also improved with eye drops and pills. Although 10 percent of normal vision seems hardly functional, it was enough to enable him see what was going on.

Vision wasn't something Harry could count on. When the pressure in his eyes increased, which would happen without warning, his vision would become cloudy. The cloud was like fog on a windshield.

"Harry always had to be protected. We didn't want to injure his eyes any further or break his glasses," says Harry's younger brother Dennis. "But we were normal, energetic boys and we got away with the usual roughhousing. You know, we all had our share of the occasional broken tooth or banged head."

Harry would sometimes be left out because of his eye troubles, says his younger sister Joanne, who still shares the family house near Ocean Beach with Harry. "But he'd play with us, too. In fact, he'd make up the games. One was called Witcholo Patcholi. Harry played a mummy, and we'd crawl up on the rafters and wait for him to come to life and chase us around the house. He was the most creative of all of us. He built stilts and made skateboards before there were skateboards. He'd take an old seat from a broken chair and balance it on a roller skate, and we'd zip along the basement holding onto the clotheslines."

Dennis also remembers Harry as having the mechanical mind in the family. "Once he froze string in some ice and tied the ends to a camera that he had attached to a kite. When then the ice melted, the string pulled the shutter and the camera went off. He was always building something. Even now, when I get stuck, I can go to Harry and he'll figure out a solution"

Harry's daredevil streak was apparent, even at an early age. "Once he built a coaster and we dragged it up the 47th Avenue Hill," says Joanne. "And in San Francisco, the hills are like mountains to kids. We went down that hill tumbling over and over. I had my best coat on and it got caught in the wheels and was ripped to shreds."

When his eyes were too blurred to see a football or a baseball coming his way, Harry tried basketball. "I thought, 'I can't do anything wrong shooting free throws in the back yard.' I was out there one day playing and the ball bounced off the rim, came down like this," Harry says, pointing at his eyes, "and off went a $40 pair of glasses. That's when my dad said, 'If you're going to play basketball, leave the glasses inside.' Then I just aimed at the blob out there."

When Harry was seven or eight, his vision began to deteriorate even further, and the protective shell tightened around him. Harry was encouraged to stay inside, listen to the radio, to be quiet and safe.

"My dad was very set in his ways, very old country,"

says Nancy of their father, Peter Cordellos, who grew up in Greece, in the small village of Zante. "We were a very close-knit family, but for Harry, it was stifling, almost crippling, to be so dependent."

Like many people, Harry's parents couldn't imagine a world where the blind could lead normal, active lives. Throughout history, the sightless have been considered helpless, capable of existing only through the benevolence of others. During the Middle Ages, writes Donald D. Kirtley in his book, *The Psychology of Blindness,* the blind were homeless, wandering beggars. Today, attitudes towards the sightless have improved, but, as a group, the blind still occupy a stereotyped position in society.

"I went to the eye doctor one day while I was still in high school, and the receptionist wanted to know if I would like a white cane. I went home and cried," Harry says.

"We had always been told that the blind are pitifully afflicted. The only blind people I ever saw were on the street playing accordions. My mother would say, 'Oh, look at that pitiful man over there. He's blind.' I never understood what they were doing with those canes. They'd poke them out, and I figured they were groping in a world of darkness. It was so terrible to be blind. I didn't want to look like them.

"I never realized I was blind myself, legally. My parents conditioned me to be afraid of that bad word, but only because of ignorance. I think they felt there was a shame in somebody who was brought into the world blind."

In a tragic twist of fate, Harry's father had to grapple not only with his son's blindness, but also with his own. In his later years, diabetes had weakened Peter Sr.'s sight to the point where he could no longer read the numbers on bingo cards during the family's Sunday afternoon games.

"I had a braille bingo card, and I told him, 'Why don't you learn just 10 digits in braille. Then you can play by touch and you won't have to strain your eyes,'" Harry says. "That was like stabbing him in the heart. He said, 'When I can't see anymore, I don't want to play anymore.'"

The day of his daughter Nancy's wedding in 1968, a massive diabetic hemorrhage decimated Peter Sr.'s remaining vision. "He just gave up. The last two years of his life, he would just sit on the chair day in and day out and listen to soap operas," says Harry. "If someone came to the house, he'd let my mother help him as far as the hallway, but he wanted to walk into the front room himself. Everyone knew he had a vision problem, but the word 'blind' was something he couldn't deal with."

Harry's father passed away two years later, in November 1970. His mother, Myrtle, lived with Joanne and Harry at the family's Ocean Beach home until her death in July 1989.

In the 1940s, career opportunities for the visually impaired revolved around menial labor: broom making, basketry, chair caning, piano tuning. The public education system was similarly limiting. Most teachers and administrators were trained to give those with physical or learning disabilities basic skills, not to push for high achievement. Through junior high school, Harry was enrolled in a state sight-saving program for the visually impaired, offered at a school across town from his home.

"We had tilting-top desks to give us the proper angle of light. We had green walls, green chalkboards, special black pencils, manila paper, large-print typewriters and chalk about *that* big around," says Harry, making a circle with his thumb and forefinger.

"We had a state law that prohibited homework because we wouldn't have all these special conditions at home. Isn't that a dream for kids?" laughs Harry. "I was driven to and from school every day in a taxicab with other handicapped kids, and I couldn't get into any after-school activities because I had to leave early to catch the taxi. I had no concept of how to get around the city on a bus. When I missed the cab once or twice, I went bawling my eyes out to the vice-principal, and had to sit there until 5 p.m. when he could drive me home."

The program may have been easier on Harry's eyes, but he felt pigeonholed by the special treatment. Every time he wanted to try something new, he had to wait for approval. When he wanted to play in the band, the eye specialist had to write a letter stating that reading the music wouldn't strain his eyes. The family physician had to agree that playing the saxophone wouldn't be a strain on his heart condition. And the ear specialist had to agree that blowing on an instrument wouldn't force too much air into his ears.

"It was more trouble than it was worth," Harry says. "And when I went into the shop classes, same thing. They only allowed me to use hand tools. Whenever I went into the shop with power tools, the teacher would bark, 'Do you see that line on the floor? Don't come across it, we've got the band saw going!' If he thought I couldn't see the saw, how could he expect me to see the line on the floor? It was ridiculous."

Fortunately, by the time Harry graduated from Everett Junior High School in 1952, his eyes had improved significantly.

"The doctor said he'd like me to try going to regular classes because no one was going to wait on me hand and foot after I graduated from high school. My teachers and parents worried that I would damage my eyesight doing the heavy amounts of reading and homework required of regular students, but there was no way I would turn down such an opportunity. I couldn't wait. I would be attending George Washington High School, known nationally for its outstanding scholastic achievements, athletic accomplishments, and school spirit. Just being part of such a school was enough to get me motivated from the first day."

Harry followed his older brother Peter to Washington High. But the two didn't interact much. Peter, a track and football star, spent most of his time on the playing field.

"When Harry got to Washington High, he was 5'2" and 125 pounds," Peter says. "When he graduated, he was 6 feet and still 125 pounds. People didn't believe he was my brother."

Both Peter and Dennis were elected outstanding athletes of their class. Nancy and Joanne also were active in sports. Harry just didn't fit.

A scrawny, fragile kid with a heart murmur and weak eyes, Harry stayed on the sidelines of activity in school. Whether he liked it or not, he was excused from physical education classes. The closest he got to participating in sports was handing out towels in the locker room or sitting in the stadium bleachers.

"He was sunken-chested, round shouldered, thin, tall, and gangly, because he was restricted from any physical activity," says Nancy.

Such a description is hard to picture looking at Harry now. Lean, muscular, shoulders back and head high, Harry looks the consummate athlete.

"The joke of the family is that the two brothers who won the Senior Athlete of the Year awards in high school are now 200 pounds overweight, and Harry has run more than 100 marathons and is still going strong," brother Dennis laughs.

At lunch hour in high school, Harry would head for his favorite spot—the top of the school stadium. He would gaze across the field at the panoramic view of the city and the Golden Gate Bridge spanning the entrance to the San Francisco Bay. Harry couldn't see well enough to pinpoint cars on the bridge, but the sunstruck windshields flashed like jewels in between the majestic cable towers. He fantasized about getting hold of a football and running up and down the field, daring the opposition to catch him.

"I figured this was only a dream, that I could never go anywhere in the sports world with such limited eyesight," says Harry, smiling at how the years have changed his perspective.

"I liked it up there in the stadium because somehow or other I was determined that the athletic field, in some way, shape, or form, would eventually play an important part in my life."

Within a few months of starting high school, Harry's vision took a dive. Before his first year was over he had undergone two operations, which improved his sight for the short term. But the tell-tale signs of glaucoma returned with increasing frequency. The blurry fog and the colored halos around lights and windows made it difficult for Harry to function as a sighted student.

"My eyes felt like rocks in my head at times," he says. Harry took prescription drugs and put drops in his eyes daily to keep the pressure down, but by fourth period, the medicine would wear off and the afternoon would turn into a blur.

Harry's grades jumped all over the scale. He had a head for math, but couldn't read the trigonometry tables. He received straight A's in composition and spelling, but flunked literature courses because he couldn't see well enough to read the words. "I was just surviving. I faked my way through a lot of it, and told teachers that I had medicine in my eyes to get excused from quizzes."

In band class, Harry memorized all the music by ear. He could rarely see writing on the page, much less notes on the staff. But he would pretend to read the music to try and hide his disability from the other students.

"One day we were practicing 'The Star Spangled Banner' for a football game. When the director stopped to correct someone, the girl sitting next to me said, 'Do you always play with the music upside down?' I made a joke and flipped the paper over. 'C'mon now,' she said, 'I didn't say backwards!'

"There was no way I could figure out which way the music was supposed to go, so I just bumped the music stand and knocked the sheet to the floor. The girl beside me, very much annoyed, picked it up and put it back. I assumed it faced the right way, but I wouldn't have known otherwise."

A smart, shy, rather quiet kid, Harry couldn't bring himself to admit to his sight problems or talk to anyone about his fears—even if asking for help meant smoothing the way for himself. He was afraid of being teased, afraid of being sent back to the sight-saving classes.

"We never knew how bad it was for him in school—all the ridicule he took, and how he couldn't even see to get to class," Dennis says. "I didn't understand how his eyes could be okay one minute and then foggy the next. I wondered if he was faking it.

"Even now, Harry does so many things, you feel he's almost sighted. My nine-year-old daughter had a bunch of red, white, and blue balloons. She mixed them up and he guessed the colors—and got them right. She said, 'Are you really blind?' Now Harry's comfortable with it. But in high school, he never talked about it. He wanted to be like the rest of us."

Harry had only one goal in high school: to graduate.

"It was an obsession with me, to get that diploma in spite of what was going on with my eyes," he remembers. And Harry was smart enough and creative enough to get through. But at what price?

"It was miserable having one close call after another," he says. "But there was something that made me believe that this nightmare of fear would not be the end result. I knew without a doubt that God was there. It wasn't that somebody had to tell me, 'have faith, have faith.' I just had this feeling inside that as long as I didn't give up, He was not going to give up."

Harry persevered and graduated from Washington High in 1955. He was proud—and relieved—to have made it through. But instead of standing on a springboard to the future, Harry felt more isolated and directionless than ever. He never would have believed that 20 years later, he'd be invited into the high school's Hall of Fame, along with the likes of Johnny Mathis.

Harry's high school counselors often had asked him about plans for a job after graduation. But he put off any decisions, reasoning that he should wait until after his next eye operation.

"I'd tell them, 'When my eyes are better, then we can decide.' The counselors were just as sympathetic as my parents were, so rather than being stern about facing reality, they let me slide," Harry says. "I got out of high school with absolutely no preparation."

Harry spent the summer after graduation sitting around the house, listening to radio soap operas. At noon, he would go down to his father's Ocean Beach restaurant, Pete's Place, to wash dishes. "Each day was the same. I was in a terrible rut, but I didn't know what else to do."

Harry hated working at the restaurant. Messy dishes didn't bother him, but he couldn't stand cigarette smoke or ashes. His eyesight was so poor that he invariably put his hands in the ashes that had been dumped on the dishes. Not only was it a health risk for customers, but also for Harry, who eventually lost one of his eyes because of infection from second-hand smoke.

In December 1956, Harry went in for his thirteenth eye operation. The doctors had told him that there was no hope of improving his eyesight and only a small chance of saving what little vision remained. The surgery went smoothly, but the next afternoon Harry felt an explosion of pain in his left eye, as if someone had stuck a knife in and then twisted it.

Harry's doctor told him that one of the chambers in his eye had collapsed.

"I was suddenly hit with the realization that my eye had failed completely. I was totally blind in the left eye!" Then Harry's right eye began to sympathize with the left, a common phenomenon in ophthalmology. Now, Harry's sight was worse than ever; he could see little more than light and shadow. He couldn't even see well enough to wash dishes at Pete's Place.

He spent hours at the restaurant, sitting quietly in the end seat at the horseshoe-shaped counter or leaning idly against the coffee urn.

"It was sad to see him in my Dad's restaurant," Nancy says. "He'd be there by the hour, dreaming, a million miles away. Harry had a sharp, sharp mind and an exceptional imagination. It was a waste."

For more than two years, Harry was trapped in emotional and physical lethargy. He couldn't function as a sighted person, and he was ignorant of the opportunities for the blind. Indeed, Harry still didn't think of himself as blind. He thought that meant a world of unbearable darkness.

"A customer came into the restaurant and plunked some change down on the stainless steel counter," says Harry's brother, Peter. "Harry couldn't see the coins and asked the man to pay. 'What's the matter,' the man responded, 'Are you blind?' Harry was crushed. He went in the back and cried."

Harry hit rock bottom. He was withdrawn and depressed. Unable to read the newspaper or watch television, he immersed himself in the fantasy world of radio soap operas.

"While I didn't realize it at the time, I was very close to a mental breakdown," he says. "I thought about suicide, but I knew that if I were to take my own life, I would be denying my belief that God was there to help. That was never in question."

Then, just before Christmas 1957, a dinner-table conversation opened a door that would turn Harry's life around. Lee Vavuris was a close family friend and often stopped by Pete's Place with his wife. One night, the subject of Harry's future came up, and Lee, who was recovering from a long bout with pulmonary tuberculosis, talked about the California Department of Vocational Rehabilitation. Neither Harry nor his parents had ever heard about such a place. They listened with growing excitement as Lee talked about the program, which offered training for the disabled to pursue a college education or a career.

"It seemed crazy," Harry says. "What kind of magic act could they pull off? I couldn't travel anywhere alone, much less go to college and be a successful student. But if the program could do half as much for me as Lee promised, I would actually start to live life instead of just existing from day to day."

That night, Harry looked through the restaurant windows towards the ocean. His eyes were just clear enough to see the bright orange-gold glow of the sun as it sank beneath the ink-blue horizon. It was a beautiful sight. He thought of it as a symbol, a beginning.

"SUNSET"

When I am walking on the beach
Along the edge of town,
I like to pause when day is done
To watch the sun go down.
To me, it's like a chest of gold
That sends us sparkling glares.
The swells that rise before it
Make it rest on golden stairs.
The mystery of the treasure chest
Is one I'll never know,
For when it's there, the western sky
Is captured by its glow.
It seems to stand completely still,
But yet, it slips away.
And though it's swallowed by the sea,
It still returns each day.

One day, I watched a sailing ship
Move swiftly toward the west
To try before the end of day
To seize the treasure chest.
But way out there where sky meets sea,
The sun was sinking low.
The ship became a silhouette
Before the fading glow.
The cliffs that once were gleaming gold
Were now a bluish gray.
Above, the stars began to peep
As daylight passed away.
And now, the golden stairs were gone,
The treasure gone as well.
The sky grew dark and peaceful
As the evening shadows fell.

—Harry Cordellos

Chapter 2

STEP INTO THE WORLD

"When a person comes to us, the need is a two-fold one: to learn skills and to develop a conviction and a feeling of confidence, something deep in his soul that he knows basically he's the same person blind as if he weren't blind."
—Allen Jenkins, Administrator,
Orientation Center for the Blind, Albany. Ca.

For people who can see, blindness seems like falling into a dark hole: Close your eyes and the world becomes a threatening void, an emptiness that presses in. A sighted person relies on eyes to negotiate the complex path through life, in, around, over, through things. Imagine what it's like not to have that ability. Without sight, a person is physically isolated, trapped in the dark, in a disorienting nightmare maze of doorways, curbs, tree branches, eating utensils, traffic, noise and odors. Right?

Not exactly. Being blind isn't like turning the lights off and groping helplessly in the dark. A reporter once asked Harry, who had just crossed the finish line of his first marathon, what it was like to run 26 miles in total darkness. "I don't know," he said. "I don't think anyone in their right mind would run in darkness."

Harry describes his blindness as trying to look out the back of your head. "What do you see?" he asks. "It's not light, it's not dark. It's certainly not blackness. You visualize colors, or the wall you're running your finger along, or cars going by."

When the optic nerve is stimulated, the brain interprets that as light. If that nerve is gone or damaged, the eye doesn't pick up any more light than the end of the finger does, according to Allen Jenkins, head administrator at the Orientation Center for the Blind in Albany, California. "If you put your finger out there to see if it's light or dark, your finger doesn't know. When you get accustomed to being blind, it's like not being able to fly. You just work out other ways of doing things."

Mike McAviney, one of Harry's classmates at the orientation center, is even more the concise realist when it comes to blindness. "It's like having a headache. It's a pain in the butt," says Mike, who is one of Harry's regular companions in snow skiing, water-skiing, and running. "I've learned to live with it. I don't make a big fuss over it."

Sounds simple enough. With the right attitude, adjusting to blindness is much the same as learning to fix cars or becoming fluent in a new language. But there's a psychological component, too. After high school, Harry desperately needed training, not only in how to act blind, but also in how to think blind.

The first task in coming to grips with blindness is to figure out how to do all those things that other people do using their eyes: reading, writing, telling time, dialing the phone, cooking, walking across the street, taking the bus, matching socks. Some activities take a bit of skill and technique to work out, others can be accomplished with common sense.

Then there's the other side of blindness, that has little to do with logistics or any physical impairment.

"It has to do with the age-old, and still world-wide, range of conceptions, or more properly, misconceptions, that people have about what blindness means," says Allen Jenkins. "All too often a blind person shares those same stereotypical ideas about incompetence and being regarded as a lesser person because he is blind."

Allen himself lost his sight at age 8 when he fell through a glass window playing at his home in Texas. His parents enrolled him in a state school for the blind. "They put me in a room with 28 or 30 other boys, many of whom were obviously retarded. The school people talked to me in a very hopeful way about teaching me piano tuning, basketry, chair caning, broom making," Allen remembers.

"They called this the 'Opportunity Room.' I was depressed without quite knowing why. They saw what they were offering me in terms of great hope; I determined the first day that I didn't want to stay there."

During lunch hour, he dug his way under a hedge, climbed over a fence, and hitchhiked a few hundred miles home, telling drivers that his bus ticket had expired and the aunt and uncle he had been visiting in Austin didn't have enough money to buy him a new one. That escapade was enough to convince his parents that he could handle just about anything, including public schools.

Allen went on to study law and advise California state legislators on policies for the blind. In 1951 he was asked to help develop a skills training and adaptive orientation program for the blind. At age 28, he became the youngest director of a state agency—the head administrator of the California Orientation Center for the Blind. Now, at age 70, with graying hair and craggy face, he is still in the administrator's chair, feet up on his desk—and he's one of the oldest directors of a state agency.

"What we expect for the person to do when he leaves here is to go out and fulfill his desires in life, much in the same manner as other people do," says Allen. "We have had people without much in the way of opportunity come here and be encouraged to go out and do things they didn't dream would be possible even when they had vision."

Harry certainly fit that slice of the population. "He came in without ambition, without hope," Allen remembers.

The first question Harry got from his counselor at the Department of Rehabilitation was, "How long have you been blind?" Harry of course bristled at the label. "Blind? I could still see a little, so I thought he had made a mistake," says Harry. "But I was so depressed at that point, I figured if this guy wants to call me blind, let him call me whatever he wants. I'll go make a mess of the orientation center and they'll realize that I'm not blind after all."

Without meaning to, Harry had half his problem licked. His counselor had deliberately called him blind to get a reaction. It's not at all uncommon for people with even profoundly limited vision to resist the label. "Blind" has a finality to it that is difficult for most people to accept. But even if it was out of resignation, Harry hadn't corrected his counselor. He knew that he could no longer try to go through life as a sighted person. What Harry didn't quite realize was that he was signing up for a nine-month course in becoming a blind man.

The center was on the other side of the San Francisco Bay, almost an hour's drive from Harry's home. He had never been away from his family before, even for a few days. He couldn't imagine what it would be like to live with a bunch of blind people. Harry's family couldn't understand, either. A clothing salesclerk asked Harry's mother what the special occasion was for buying him new clothes. Harry overheard as his mother leaned over the counter and whispered, "He's going into the Home for the Blind."

When he went to tour the center, Harry smelled broom corns as he walked up the path to the main entrance. All the stereotypes came flooding back. He wondered if his mother was right, that he was being relegated to a rest home for the blind, a place where people did nothing all day but make brooms.

Allen Jenkins quickly put that fear to rest, telling Harry that the broom factory had nothing to do with the orientation program. The only shop work for Harry would be in class, learning to use a radial saw, a band saw, a drill press—all the tools he had been itching to get his hands on, and prohibited from touching because of his sight limitations.

When Harry's parents took him to the center to start the program, one of the students took the three on a tour of the facility. First stop was the woodworking shop.

"We were all kind of scared about it. Everybody in the shop was blindfolded. Whether or not they were totally blind, they certainly could not see the teeth of those saws inches away from their fingers," Harry says. "Somebody turned on the radial arm saw, and it went

Whoooooooooshshsh! I thought someone was going to scream at any minute that they lost their arm. No one cut their hand off then, and they haven't since.

"The last thing my Dad told me when they left me in the dormitory was, 'Now I don't want you in that shop. You're not going to be a cabinetmaker, that's just a waste of your time. Learn the things that you have to learn here so you can get out and come home again.' His idea was that I'd be living with him the rest of my life. I couldn't wait until he got out the door so I could go down and talk to the shop teacher. I was like a bird turned loose out of a cage."

It was mid-July 1958, when Harry's parents said goodbye and drove back across the Bay Bridge to cool, foggy San Francisco. Harry's first stop was not the shop, but the mobility training office, where he was fitted with his first white cane and a pair of welders' goggles which would blot out the little vision that still remained.

Now Harry was indeed in total blackness. Rather than relying on the small amount of remaining vision for cues, it was time for Harry to develop his other senses so he could touch, hear, smell his way around.

Within the first 10 minutes as a totally blind person, Harry had a headache and was dizzy and nauseous. His reaction wasn't uncommon; it is tremendously disorienting to be suddenly deprived of sight. Even though Harry could see little before, now he had no horizon, no light or shadow on which to focus.

"Just walking around the building gave me a very uneasy feeling. All those everyday sounds I had never listened to seemed so strange mixed with the rhythmic clicking of canes on the floors of the building," Harry remembers. "I felt the urge to laugh, but nothing was really funny.

"It reminded me of when my eyes were so bad a few years earlier. I couldn't play tag unless we played blind tag at night with the lights out, and everyone tied a dish towel around their heads and groped and chased each other by sound. Only now it was for real."

Harry's nervous impulse to laugh at all the new sounds and sensations quickly vanished as he got to work learning the cane techniques. He started out on the sidewalk in front of the center, simply talking about traffic and sounds with his instructor. Within a few weeks he had progressed from walking up and down the sidewalk to traveling around the block. Then he tried crossing streets, then streets with electric traffic signals. Then is was time to conquer a real "monster," as Harry puts it—MacArthur Boulevard. The boulevard had traffic signals, right turn lanes, center dividers and islands, and off-angle intersections. He negotiated these difficulties successfully, building up his confidence enormously.

One weekend, Harry decided it was time to test his fledgling travel skills by going home—on his own. That's no easy task when it involves bridges, bus transfers, and snarled traffic. He took two buses into San Francisco, carefully monitoring turns, major intersections, and speed to keep track of his location. He could easily tell when they crossed the Bay Bridge and swung wide to the left to go through the Yerba Buena tunnel. He noticed the clunk of the bus going over the expansion joints at the bridge towers. In San Francisco, he boarded a bus for Ocean Beach, recognizing the steep incline of the city's hills and, finally, the smell of hamburgers, hot dogs and popcorn at Playland-at-the-Beach. Harry's skill at knowing where he is and remembering descriptions of places has only improved over the years. It's uncanny the way he gives precise directions to drivers or points out scenery along a race route.

When Harry arrived unannounced that day at his father's restaurant, there was enthusiastic family pandemonium. They couldn't believe he had traveled across the Bay by himself. Harry couldn't stop talking about the center and all the new things he was experiencing.

Harry's parents were proud of their son's new-found independence, but also a bit befuddled. One weekend, his mother was on the phone with an uncle and Harry overheard her say in surprise, "And can you believe it, he actually likes it over there!"

"He'd come home on the bus by himself," remembers Joanne. "Then I'd walk him down to the restaurant, and he'd say, 'No, no, don't touch me!' I was so proud that Harry could now use a cane and get around by himself."

Harry's rehabilitation counselor at the orientation center suggested getting a dog guide, which could give him even more independence. It's an option that comes up still. But Harry wants to stick with his cane. "It's much more flexible for my needs. With all the stuff I do, where would I park a dog? There are dogs that have run marathons, but their pads are not made to run 26 miles on pavement."

Besides, says Harry, he might get too attached to a dog. "I know what it's like when we have lost cats of our own. You feel really sad. Imagine losing an animal that is more than a pet. He's a part of your life."

Harry's new mode of travel certainly wasn't the only skill he picked up at the orientation center. He re-learned reading and writing, using the raised-dot system developed by Louis Braille in France in the early 1800s. It can be a frustrating and slow process, learning to sensitize the fingers to "read" as letters groups of pin-prick-sized bumps. And it is far more time-consuming than using sight. But instead of relying on someone to read to him, Harry could now forge his way through books and magazines by touch. Harry learned to use a Braille typewriter, as well as a conventional typewriter.

During Harry's time at the center, computers were still a space-age fantasy. Now there are machines that take a print book and convert it into braille, as well as computers with voice synthesizers to "read" braille and print. But high-tech advances haven't gotten students off the hook in learning the basics.

Henry Kruse, former mayor of Albany, teaches students at the center to handle their business, legal, and financial affairs. His favorite machine? The abacus. "Braille is a little awkward with arithmetic," says Henry, who was born blind. "The abacus is the world's second oldest computer—right after the fingers—and I think it's the best."

For any blind person, a big step towards independence happens when they master the kitchen. It's difficult to rely on someone else to do all the cooking; but, without eyes, a kitchen is a minefield: There are hot burners, sharp knives, complex appliances. And how to read a recipe? Figure out what's in the drawers and cabinets? Set the oven at the proper temperature? It's surprisingly uncomplicated. With the use of braille labels and raised dots on appliance controls, Harry learned to get around the kitchen with his fingertips. Recipes, of course, are printed in braille.

Twice each week, he and his classmates would plan and prepare a meal to share with fellow students, rather than eating in the center's dining room. Cooking isn't a skill that Harry has kept up; living with his sister Joanne means that he gets her home cooking every night. But the lessons weren't lost on Harry: He adapted the technique of using braille labels for shutter and focus markers on a camera when he later took up photography.

People ask Harry all the time if he really is blind. He just seems too comfortable walking, talking, eating, and giving directions to be without eyesight. Of course, that's a sighted person's perspective. "I am most definitely blind," Harry laughs. But he also takes it as a compliment to his training.

Living-skills class at the center taught Harry all kinds of awareness tricks. Little things—social etiquette, table manners, clothing, grooming, handling money—contribute to a person's image. Blind people who have had no adaptive training sometimes twitch or rock back and forth, or tilt their heads to one side. Not Harry. When he eats, he does use his hands to figure out if there's more food on the plate, or to find the pile of catsup for his French fries. He gropes around a bit to find his coffee cup. But he's subtle and quite fastidious. He rarely spills anything.

Harry folds his $10 bills in half and his $20 bills in thirds, so that he knows how much he's handing to the cashier. He's also learned an efficient system for clothing: He sticks to basic colors for easy matching and wears light colors for better visibility at night. Harry decided that his wardrobe was going to be light gray and blue, and is still adamant about it. Joanne, rolling her eyes, tells of the time when Harry received a shirt for his birthday and wanted a description of it.

"Mama said, 'It's light gray, Harry, just the color you wanted.' He said, 'It's plain?' It had just a fine stripe in it; you could hardly see it." But Harry got out his opticon, a device that reads patterns and traces it by vibration on to his hand. "He went over the shirt and found out that the stripe was wider than Mama said. You can't pull one over on Harry. He's fussy."

Harry was like a sponge at the orientation center, soaking up every experience and every tidbit of information. Shop class gave him something more than a new skill; it was a breakthrough in confidence.

The first time he walked into shop class, he was eager to get at the power tools. The equipment does not have special adaptations for the blind, and he wondered how students managed to keep their fingers and hands intact. The shop instructor, Everett Whitney, had a foolproof safety method: using common sense, and understanding the machinery before trying to use it.

First Harry learned to use hand tools to saw and plane wood into straight, square blocks. Then he tried the drill press. Instead of using pencil marks—which of course blind students couldn't see—Whitney showed Harry how to use a center punch to mark where to drill a hole. Harry could feel the depression in the wood with his fingertips, and with the power still off, guide the drill bit to the wood.

He turned the power on and drilled a perfect hole.

The next day, Whitney suggested it was time to tackle the table saw.

"Right in front of me was a circular blade with some of the most wicked-looking teeth one could ever see or feel. They were so sharp," Harry remembers. "For almost 20 years I had been told terrible tales of how people had lost their hands and fingers in power saws."

But with Whitney guiding his hands, Harry learned

about each part of the machine, and where his hands would be in relation to each of the moving parts. His first task was to cut a two-inch piece off a block of wood. He tried the sequence with the power off, then used a braille ruler to measure the distance from the rip-cutting fence to the blade. With Whitney behind him, Harry flicked the power switch.

"The wood wasn't touching the blade, but the noise sounded horrible. It was frightening," Harry says. "As I pushed the wood and safety guard into contact with the saw, I heard Whit say, 'Stay in control. Hold down tight and push through steadily. Don't be afraid, you're doing fine.'

"I felt calmer then, but the closer I got to sawing through the wood, the more horrifying it seemed. I could feel the wind from the saw teeth blowing over my fingers, and sharp splinters of wood flew back, hitting my fingers and arm. Suddenly the saw stopped grating."

He had cut through the block. Harry brought the wood and guard back to the starting point, turned off the power and pushed the choke slowly toward the saw to stop the blade from rotating.

"I reached for the piece that I had cut and held it up to the braille ruler: two inches exactly."

Harry didn't have time to bask in his accomplishment. Next came the wood lathe, then the band saw, the jointer, the sander, and the radial arm saw. He was in craftsman heaven. The fruits of his labor still decorate the family home: a salad bowl made from lathed pieces of wood, a glass-top coffee table, a folding picnic table, a guitar with intricate inlay and smooth, graceful curves.

"He was quite good in the shop," Allen Jenkins remembers. "He made a merry-go-round arrangement run with a clever electric motor."

The merry-go-round project blossomed into a passion for Harry. He turned his mechanical skills to building a whimsical and elaborate carnival display, complete with moving parts, lights, and music. There's a 20-inch Ferris wheel, a parachute jump with riders bouncing on rubber bands, a diving bell with a cake-plate pool and a medicine-jar bell. Birthday-cake-decoration dancers twirl round and round on the ice. The tilt-a-whirl motion is so realistic that Harry had to use paper-clip restraining devices to keep the pipe cleaner riders in their seats. The carnival, powered by a single motor and fishing wire, goes on display every year during the holidays. It's his way of paying tribute to Playland-at-the-Beach, the San Francisco amusement park that was a centerpiece in his childhood. He was always too scared and frail to go on the rides before the place was demolished. Now he's got his own mini-version.

The thought of Harry using power tools was too nerve-wracking for his mother, who refused to allow them in the house. After she passed away, Harry and family friend, Joe Giammattei, set up a shop in a tidy corner of the garage. The two spend time down there tinkering away. "I just love anything mechanical," Harry says, smiling.

Less than two weeks after Harry enrolled at the orientation center, Everett Whitney, the shop instructor, organized a camping and water-skiing trip for the 35 students to Don Pedro Lake in the foothills of California's Sierra Nevada mountains.

Water-skiing? Blind? No way. Harry couldn't even swim.

"I had almost drowned in a motel swimming pool a month earlier," Harry recalls. "I had jumped into the deep water, become totally disoriented, and had to be fished out of the pool by the lifeguard."

When he had had better vision, Harry had seen water-skiers in a movie on a gigantic Cinerama screen. "How could anyone in their right mind be dragged along behind a boat at such high speeds, and then be plunged into the water? It looked like suicide to me," he remembers.

But sleeping under the stars sounded like a fun—and much safer—adventure.

When the group arrived on a hot, dry, Friday afternoon, Harry went to look at Whit's power boat. Up close, he could see that the hull was white and deck bright red. The boat's name, "Hit it!" was painted on the stern. "That's what Whit wants to hear when you're ready to ski," one of the instructors said. But Harry wasn't even sure he wanted to ride *in* the boat, much less bounce along in its wake.

Harry watched and listened as the other blind students took their turn on skis, surprised at how many got up on the water. He could hear a lot of loud splashes and spills and friendly laughter. Whit offered the rope handle to Harry, who shook his head. He wanted to try, but was afraid. The closest he got to the boat was to put on a life preserver and paddle around close to the lake shore.

But Harry didn't like missing out on an activity that was giving everyone else such a charge. He wondered what the others thought of his unwillingness to give it a try. His pride was piqued, when he heard all the women in the group going for it while he was hanging back. Whit sensed that Harry's enthusiasm was tempered by fear, and didn't let him off the hook.

"You've got the life jacket on. Guess you're next, Harry!" he prodded, tossing him the rope. Harry didn't have time to refuse. With the life preserver keeping his shoulders and chin out of the water, Harry put the skis on his feet and took hold of the tow line. Harry thought he was nuts for getting himself into such a predicament, then heard himself yell, "Hit it!"

"A large wall of water rushed toward me as the line tightened. I dropped below the surface for a moment and the ski handle jerked out of my hand. Whit circled the boat around. 'You leaned back too far,' he yelled to me. 'Take your time and relax.'"

Harry's second and third attempts were no more successful. On the fourth try, Harry's skis began to rise out of the water, then fell back again. He knew he could do it if he just weren't so scared of falling.

That night, Harry found himself in a new world. Instead of the concrete, loud buses, and smelly exhaust of the city, Harry discovered mountain air, trees, and wildlife.

"The night was filled with sounds I had never noticed before. There were crickets, crawling animals, buzzing things, and the lapping of the water on the shore. One of our group was playing a harmonica, and another was playing a guitar and singing."

During a midnight boat ride, the full moon cast a

silver path of light across the lake. Harry could see the intense contrast between the black sky and the moon glow. He heard the rushing water of the dam. "I dangled my arm over the side of the boat and felt the warm water slipping past," Harry says. "Nothing compared with the beauty of being close to nature that night."

Harry awoke to the sound of birds chattering, the smell of camp-stove coffee, and the feel of the sun on his face. He was itching to get back on those water-skis.

Soon enough, he was in the water yelling the familiar, "Hit it!" He gripped the tow bar and watched as the wall of water in front of him parted and his skis skimmed the lake surface.

"I saw my hands on the rope handle, and beyond that, a golden pathway of light on the water as we glided along towards the sun. I couldn't have been happier. I knew that pathway of light was leading me to a new way of life that would be richer and more meaningful than all the gold in the world."

In a flicker, blindness suddenly lost its stranglehold on Harry. "I was thinking, 'Blind and water-skiing? How silly.' Blind is such a threatening word, but it was falling away from me as fast as I was moving away from the shore. If I could water-ski, I could do anything. Sure, there are modified ways you have to do things. But if you're willing to go for it, there really is no limit."

Mike McAviney, one of Harry's water-skiing compadres that day at Don Pedro, remembers a dramatic shift in Harry's attitude from "cautious and careful" to "try anything." For Mike, whose upbringing was a stark contrast to Harry's, the orientation program was more like summer camp.

After Mike was born with cataracts, his parents enrolled him as a child in the state's only residential school for the blind, in Berkeley, California. "My parents thought blindness shouldn't stop me from anything," says 54-year-old McAviney, who now works in customer relations at IBM near Denver, Colorado.

"When I lost my sight completely at age 14, I was devastated. I locked myself in my room for three days.

My dad grabbed me by the ears and said, 'You have a life to lead. Get your butt out there. You might skin your knees a few times, but experience is the best teacher.' They gave me no slack, and I'm forever grateful for that."

Mike went to regular public high school and enrolled at the orientation center between his junior and senior year. He already had good skills in mobility and a solid foundation in braille and in living skills.

But for Harry, says Mike, training at the center was the keystone in building a new life. "His folks had discouraged everything he wanted to do—out of love, not meanness. He was told he had a bad heart; he was always told he might get hurt. If you're told something long enough, you'll believe it.

"That's what makes Harry's transition so remarkable. He came from a background that was limiting and rose above it. If there's a challenge there, he's willing to try. He doesn't know if he'll fail, but knows it's better to fail because of your own inability than because you don't try."

Of course, Harry never imagined just how far his new attitude would take him. "If you had told me that 28 years later I'd win a world competition in trick skiing or that I'd be skiing in the most famous water-skiing show in the world, I'd probably call for the men in the white coats to come pick you up."

Harry still talks about water-skiing the way some people talk about religion or their first love: with awe and conviction, wonder and gratitude. The sport marks such a turning point for him that he divides his life into B.W. and A.W.: Before Water-skiing and After Water-skiing. August 17, 1958, is the day Harry got up on water-skis, and it's a day that he has relived at least a thousand times. But he has made sure he didn't stop there.

"I felt like I was walking on water. But I knew it would be too easy to slip right back to where I had been in the past. Confidence and a good attitude do not automatically last forever."

For Harry, sports became synonymous with life, a way to fuel the fire of his enthusiasm. The confidence sparked by water-skiing grew with every new activity. He's determined to prove that he can stay in top shape and try the seemingly impossible not just once or twice, but every day.

Walking in the door of the orientation center was the first step to answering Harry's every hope and prayer. "For almost 20 years, I had existed much like a vegetable. But that was all behind me now. It was like being born all over again. I was ready to step into the world and live."

Chapter 3

KEEP THE FAITH

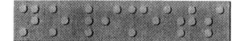

> *"When Harry was an intern at a youth recreation*
> *program in East Oakland, the kids of course thought,*
> *'Oh boy, here's a blind man, we'll get away with murder.'*
> *They tested him, sneaking from one corner of the room*
> *to the other. But they didn't know they were playing right*
> *into his strengths. He could hear them shuffle across the*
> *room, hear them giggle. They were amazed he knew*
> *their names just by knowing their voices. He did arts*
> *and crafts with them, taught them rally ping-pong,*
> *played musical instruments. Pretty soon he was*
> *like the Pied Piper of the park."*
> —Jim Battersby, former director,
> Arroyo Viejo Recreation Facility

If Harry had had his druthers, he would have spent the rest of his days behind a boat, skimming across white-capped wakes, or in the wood shop, working on crafts projects. But to his teachers and counselors at the orientation center, that was just play, and a waste of Harry's intellect and education.

The orientation center's aim was to prepare its students for college or professional careers. Harry didn't know what kind of a job he wanted, so his counselors steered him towards college as the next step. But the angst of high school had left him with a sour taste for academics. Harry just couldn't get excited about school, at least not after discovering sports. Water-skiing, bowling, now they were fun and thrilling, and a welcome ego-boost after the years of self-doubt.

"All of a sudden I had to forget about water-skiing and start thinking about studying," Harry says, his voice still revealing a trace of irritation. "It didn't seem right at all. Why should I have to give up the one single thing in my life that had given me more personal satisfaction and confidence than anything else and replace it with something as dull as reading one textbook after another?"

Back then, Harry would have scoffed at the idea that college would bolster his self-esteem even further, that he would become a college newspaper photographer, graduate with honors, and go on to pursue his master's degree.

In 1959, unfocused academically and more than a bit resentful, Harry enrolled at San Francisco City College, becoming the school's first full-time blind student.

Of course, City College couldn't offer Harry the same adaptive facilities as the orientation center, or the same kind of attention. He was entering the sighted world; instead of approaching it as a challenge, Harry looked at it as a bother. At first he grumbled about having to find readers to help him with assignments. He wondered why the school didn't have a special place for handicapped students to study. He had no idea what he wanted to study, and wasn't remotely motivated by his first-semester classes, the usual general-education requirements: English, chemistry, Spanish, and algebra.

Harry wasn't bored as much as he was scared. He couldn't help remembering the fears and failures of high school, and he was afraid that academic pressures would send him sliding back into anxiety and depression.

He thought about dropping out. Then he started meeting people whose support and friendship gave him a much-needed attitude adjustment.

Most of Harry's professors and colleagues had never worked with a blind student before, and had more questions for him than he did for them. It was a learning experience for everyone. "The attitude towards disabled students was super," Harry says. "The usual approach was, 'If there's a way to do it, we'll find it.'"

Harry bought a tape recorder for lectures and transcribed tapes into braille lecture notes. Instructors helped him find classmates willing to do textbook work with him.

Often he would sit outside with his readers, in the campus' flower-dotted courtyards. One of the campus deans found a small storage area in the library stacks for Harry to use as his personal study when the weather was cold or rainy. With the help of one of his professors, Harry soon felt as comfortable walking around City College as he did around the orientation center.

"We had quite a bit of indoctrination on location since the school is on a hill with walkways, ramps, and stairs," says Roy Burkhead, former chairman of the Health and Sciences Department. "How he kept it straight, I'll never know to my dying day. He has an incredible encyclopedia of memory in his brain. He hardly ever makes a mistake."

Math professor Evelyn Kerkhof was similarly impressed with Harry's memory. "He was discouraged about mathematics because he wasn't doing as well as he knew he should do."

Evelyn, who taught Harry algebra and trigonometry, found him to be a model of eagerness and aptitude. "He sat in the front row. He was very smart. I never had to repeat things twice.

"There are all kinds of tables for functions and equations that Harry couldn't possibly memorize, and of course, he couldn't just flip to the back of the book and look for himself," says Evelyn.

"He would tell me exactly what to do. I can picture him sitting there and telling me, 'Please look up this and this for me.' He never asked questions that weren't pertinent to the problem. I would never give him a break on tests, and he always did well. He didn't expect any advantages over anybody else."

In his second semester, Harry walked into Roy Burkhead's health-education class with the usual sense of dread. He always felt threatened by the barrage of textbooks and assignments at the beginning of a semester, and worried about how the other students and teachers would treat him. But Roy was expecting Harry, and greeted him the first day with a friendly handshake.

"From the sound of his voice above me, I knew he was very tall," says Harry. "He showed me to a seat in the front row, and for the remainder of the semester, he never bothered to show me to a seat again. He figured that I didn't really need special help."

Harry welcomed that gift of independence and ease, and for the first time, felt like one of the gang in class. It was also the first time he wasn't anxious about grades. He was too interested in the subject to worry about tests. When it was time for the mid-term, he hadn't studied. Roy read him the questions, and at the end, praised Harry for acing the exam and for his enthusiasm. His professor told him, "With that attitude, you'll do well. Just remember one thing—keep the faith."

"Keep the faith." Those three words still echo in Harry's mind. "Each time I hear them, it gives my confidence a boost when I really need it," he says.

Harry never knew that Roy had been assigned to be his parent away from home. It quickly became obvious that Harry didn't need a protector; instead, Roy became his mentor—as well as a tremendous fan.

"One of the greatest honors I ever had was to know him. The outlook I get from him is that there's nothing in life that's too great to try to accomplish," Roy says. "It ended up that he taught me so much about life. It was a marvelous experience. We had such a good rapport."

Roy still laughs about the time Harry got him lost in the library stacks. "He took me up to his study room in the stacks and shut the door. It was pitch dark in there, which of course didn't matter to Harry. I was completely lost. He had more fun with me. Eventually I gave up and he turned the lights on. He has a wonderful sense of humor, and would rather pull a joke on you than fly to the moon."

Roy's teaching—and friendship—planted a seed that would grow to great heights with Harry: to make health education and physical awareness not just a college requirement, but part of daily life.

Roy helped that seed to blossom by encouraging Harry to pursue anything and everything. Well, almost anything. The only request he ever refused Harry was to learn to throw the discus.

"I said, 'You know, Harry, not that I think you couldn't do it, but it's a lethal instrument, almost as lethal as a gun.'" Harry, of course, went on in later years to throw the discus, not just for the experience, but in competition. "It's mind-boggling," laughs Roy. "He's one for the books. How many of our faculty people will never forget him?"

"Mind-boggling" is a term one hears a lot in connection with Harry. Take his stint as a blind newspaper photographer and reporter, for example.

His avocation of photojournalism started with an English class assignment to write a research paper. Harry certainly didn't want to delve into Shakespeare or James Joyce—too much reading for his taste. The professor told him to pick something that interested him. Harry had been fascinated by photography since junior high school, when he first saw pictures developing in a darkroom. He had joined the camera club then, and had taken his Brownie camera with him to family outings and events. But his motivation waned in high school, when his vision became prohibitively blurred and dim.

His orientation center training in mechanical adaptations for the blind piqued his interest again.

"I figured if I could set the grooves on the oven to bake a cake by counting them, then I could count the grooves on the dial of a camera." Harry reasoned. "And if I could aim across MacArthur Boulevard by listening to sounds, why couldn't I put a sound picture in front of me to take a picture?"

Harry's professor was intrigued by his paper's topic, "Amateur Photography for the Blind." And his research caused ripples in the photography department when he interviewed a few professors. Instead of asking questions, Harry ended up in a heated debate over whether or not a blind person could successfully pass a City College photography course.

"I heard the words 'can't' and 'impossible' so many times," Harry remembers. "They told me that 30 percent of the students drop out of the program every year—and they could see. How could I possibly compete against such odds?"

That kind of challenge put a burr under Harry's hide. He wrote a 58-page paper for his English class, and promptly signed up for a photography course. The department heads told Harry that he would get no special privileges in the class, which was fine with him. Harry wanted a real-world scenario to find out if he could turn theories into pictures.

Harry shattered more than a few stereotypes by earning an "A" in basic photography. He then went on to take photography classes every semester at City College. He learned to use complex cameras, wrote and produced a film on photography without sight, and, as a final project, put together a slide show on the Oakland Orientation Center titled "Doorway to Opportunity." After graduation, Harry took the slide show to schools, classes, and service clubs in California and New Mexico. "Doorway to Opportunity" became the nucleus for Harry's work in motivational speaking.

Harry's photography was solid enough to earn him a spot as a reporter and photographer for the campus newspaper in his final semester. Campus reporters lugging around camera equipment and notebooks hardly earned a passing glance from students—until Harry joined their ranks.

"When I walked across the busy courtyard with a large camera and a tripod in the right hand and a white cane in the left, the situation was a little different," says Harry.

Students would stand around, gawk, and ask Harry questions. How did he know what was in front of the camera? Could he really not see anything? How could he focus? Harry invited people to peek under the black cloth to check out his aim and focus. They would peer through the viewfinder, exclaim in amazement and emerge with wide-eyed respect for Harry.

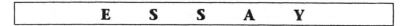

E   S   S   A   Y

"COLLEGE PHOTOGRAPHER IS COMPLETELY BLIND"
San Francisco Chronicle, 1961
by Daniel North

The power of positive thinking needs no better advocate than Harry Cordellos of City College.

Cordellos is 23, totally blind, and a top-notch student in the College Photography Department.

He is not just at home in the dark of the darkroom. He takes pictures. His work ranges from portraits to scenics to news photos for the college newspaper, *The Guardsman.*

"Confidence," says the slim, crew-cut victim of congenital glaucoma, "is the main thing, the most important thing a blind person can have..."

Since 1959, Cordellos has been totally unable to judge light or perceive objects visually.

But on a bright day he can feel the sun beat on his face and neck. On an overcast day he's aware of the sun's absence. Once he knows the exposure he wants he sets his camera by counting tiny notches on the dial containing the f-stop fixture.

"Outdoor exposure is no real problem to me, but indoors I just have to turn on all the lights and assume a constant amount of light," Cordellos says.

"As to focusing, Cordellos says, "Pacing distances has worked accurately for me. Last year I photographed the campus science building in an exercise on correcting line distortion. The picture was focused so you can count the venetian blinds.

"To center the building, I tapped against my fiberglass cane. I could tell when I was directly in front of it by the way the sound bounced off.

"I used a view camera on a tripod, and for focusing and aiming, I used a home-made plumb bob and movable notched square to adjust the camera angle and bellows length."

Cordellos' methods got results. Photography

Department head Bev Pasqualetti said his project was the best turned in by the 45-member photojournalism class.

Harry took pictures of discus throwers, hurdlers, and long-jumpers from the track team. He stood on top of chairs in the library to take publicity pictures. The dean of men volunteered to pose for him, and the result became his official photo in all the campus literature.

"When I took a portrait of someone, I would talk to the person and aim the camera according to the sound of their voice. By listening to the mood of the conversation, I could determine when to take the picture," says Harry.

It was easy enough to explain to people how he took pictures. Then the question was, why. Why bother with photography when he couldn't even enjoy the results of his labors? "It was simply a tremendous confidence builder," says Harry.

Ironically enough, photography also taught Harry something else: that he was, finally, totally blind. He was taking a picture of the science building when the realization dawned. He had set up his equipment to judge distance by sound. "It was almost as if I could see the building columns before me," he recalls. "But, at that moment, I realized I couldn't remember when I had last seen anything.

"I didn't know when I had finally lost my sight. I had been filling the gap with mental images. I never saw subjects in front of the camera; they were all in my mind's eye."

Visualization is how Harry "sees," and how he astounds people with his seemingly photographic memory. Whenever running partners describe a race route or friends tell him about a scenic view, he makes a picture of it in his mind and files it away for instant recall.

Harry left City College in 1962 with a markedly different attitude than the resentment and reluctance of three years earlier—with honors, and with a degree in education. As the recipient of the President's Award Plaque for Services, he was chosen as one of two students to speak at commencement.

"With the terrific encouragement everyone gave me here, how could I settle for Cs and Ds?" Harry asked his peers on graduation day. "All of us can conquer fear. And believe me, this faith is not something you can get by having someone else solve your problems for you."

Harry headed back to the orientation center after graduation—this time as an instructor in a volunteer internship program. He hoped a year in the teacher's training program would lead to a full-time job at the orientation center. Harry was in his element. He taught mobility classes, physical education, and home economics, and helped organize social and recreational activities. He started a weekly bowling club, and, of course, made sure the students got a chance to try their mettle on water-skis.

Harry had a ball that year. But his hopes came crashing down after a June water-skiing trip to Lake Berryessa. The center director, Jenkins, told him that the internship program would end the next month. Harry was bitterly disappointed.

"I had now had a taste of working happily and gaining great satisfaction from motivating people and watching them succeed. Why couldn't it continue?"

Employment opportunities for blind people were few and far between. Much to Harry's dismay, his counselor at City College encouraged him to return to school to finish a four-year degree to give him an educational edge over sighted job candidates.

In the fall, Harry enrolled at California State University, Hayward, and almost immediately caused some ripples. It was unusual enough to have a totally blind student. But Harry, true to form, cracked the stereotype of what blind people should and shouldn't do: he declared his major to be recreation.

"It seemed a little nutty," says Charles Buell, who was teaching physical education at the School for the Blind in Berkeley at the time, and had heard about a blind student pursuing a recreation major at Cal State. "It didn't seem like the chances of succeeding were too likely. It's hard to be able to carry on activities that you have in recreation unless you're working with someone who's sighted."

Charles himself is legally blind, but that's a far cry from the totality of Harry's lack of vision. Charles had enough sight to coach sports, and his wrestling team regularly won awards against sighted competitors. "Suppose you're working with children, and someone falls down and gets hurt or is unconscious," Charles says. "A blind person is going to be at a disadvantage, and an employer will take that into account."

But Harry didn't think that far ahead, and certainly didn't realize the difficulties he'd have in finding a job later on. All he knew in 1964 was that if more school was the answer, he was going to do it his way. In recreation, he could combine the topics and activities that had catalyzed his enthusiasm and spark: sports, health, and teaching.

At Cal State, where he was the first blind person in the recreation department, he found nothing but encouragement. "He came in with a lot of skills— photography, water-skiing, using power tools. We ended up learning from him," says Bill Niepoth, department chairman and Harry's advisor.

"I think Harry teaches all of us that we can do more than we think we can, that we can make better use of our skills. People get strength from Harry. You learn how to extend yourself, how to make the most of the talent you have."

Harry excelled in his internships, working at the Veterans Administration Hospital in Palo Alto, teaching swimming and bowling to the disabled. At the Arroyo Viejo Recreation Center in Oakland he taught craft classes to kids.

"One day Harry had the kids make butterflies out of tiles and wood and pipe cleaners," Bill said. "He moved around the room and sat down on a glued butterfly. It stuck to his pants. The kids, of course, announced it with great glee. We all laughed about that."

Harry's determination impressed everyone. "He was really excited one day and he wasn't watching where he was going," says Jim Battersby, who was his supervisor at the recreation center. "He just slammed into an oak tree and cut up his head. I would have called it a day and gone home, but he just mopped up and kept going.

"For all the successes you see, there's been 10 or 20 failures. He just gets up and goes again."

Studying recreation gave Harry what he really wanted: the opportunity to participate in sports, not just to theorize or organize for other people.

Bill Niepoth egged him into signing up for a golf class, and, after that, Harry couldn't imagine a semester going by without at least a few activity classes. By the time he was ready to graduate, he had taken classes in bowling, swimming, water safety, scuba diving, and gymnastics.

"Harry does it all. He's got a natural athletic ability," says his brother, Dennis. "He almost beat me at golf. I won't play with him anymore. How do you explain you almost got beaten by a blind person?"

Harry's family and teachers weren't the only ones impressed by his beehive energy. Monique Benott, one of the social reporters for the *San Francisco Chronicle*, asked him on a date for her daily column.

E S S A Y

"MONIQUE'S DAILY DATE: BLINDNESS DOESN'T STOP HIM"
San Francisco Chronicle, 1965
by Monique Benott

Harry Cordellos greeted me at the door of his family home, where he lives with his parents and several brothers and sisters.

Articulate and outgoing, the 28-year-old blind man has enough energy to keep several people going...

"I was told I had to go to college and get teaching credentials. I hate academic work, but I decided to give it a try."

So he enrolled at California State College in Hayward to get a B.S. in recreation.

You mean you commute every day from here on 47th Avenue?

Harry laughed: "At first I thought I wasn't going to spend three to four hours commuting, but as I wasn't sure I'd stick to my plans I didn't want to move out there, so I began going by bus.

"And do you know that I began looking forward to those bus rides? They were the only bright moments of my day.

"Those AC Transit drivers are the nicest guys; they have done more for my spirit than anyone else. Without them I think I'd have given up. Some of them even taught me to bowl."

Bowling? I was really bowled over.

"I developed a new technique using a tape that I follow with my hand."

He also casually mentioned that he goes skating.

So every morning Harry gets up at 5:45 to be in class by 8.

"On Wednesday I come home about 9 p.m. because of my swimming class in Berkeley.

"When Dale Sanders, director of the Berkeley Red Cross, heard that I went water-skiing and didn't know how to swim he thought it was pretty ridiculous. So he organized a swimming class for the blind. I am a pretty good swimmer now."

Does dating fit into that hectic schedule of yours?

"Not yet. My time, so far, has been limited, and I haven't been able to squeeze girls in, but I am graduating in June, so I'll have time for them then," said Harry, laughing.

When that happens, girls won't have to worry about sitting quietly at home.

As it turned out, Harry's "date" with Monique was one of his few ventures into the dating game. Harry's never had a girlfriend, although there are times he admittedly yearns for that kind of companionship.

Dolores Curry is one woman who saw a lot of possibility

in Harry. In 1986, while working on her master's degree at Long Beach State University, Dolores volunteered for the Blind National Championships there. She had read about Harry, and made it a point to introduce herself to the man who had impressed her in print.

"We talked a bit, then went over to the post-competition dance. We had a really great time," says 55-year-old Dolores, who now teaches speech communications at Golden West College. "The next day my girlfriend and I took Harry and his running partner, Mike Restani, to Magic Mountain."

Harry and Dolores saw each other numerous times over the next few years, and met each other's families. Harry lectured at her classes, and Dolores held a book-signing party at her house in Huntington Beach to help sell copies of his 1981 autobiography, *Breaking Through*. A few years ago, the two, along with Mike Restani, went together to the Blind National Championships in Albuquerque, New Mexico.

"It was such fun being with 200 to 300 blind athletes and seeing them perform such feats. Harry, of course, received all kinds of awards there. It was a wonderful experience.

"Mike says I'm the only woman Harry's ever had a relationship with. But it was friendship, not dating. There was no intimacy. We didn't even hold hands," Dolores says.

"He's pretty closed off. He talked about his feelings, but it was always rather superficial, talking about his family or his accomplishments.

"Maybe his way of coping and surviving with blindness is to focus on himself. So many people have done things for him for so many years, he never learned how to give to a relationship. I don't fault him for it. I think he's a phenomenal person because of his accomplishments. He's done far more than I could ever do. I'm thrilled I met him, and I loved our time together."

Nothing more ever blossomed between Harry and Dolores. The two drifted apart and haven't been in much contact in recent years.

"Harry is so wrapped up in sports and his own life, that he doesn't have time for women," says his buddy, Mike McAviney, who is married and has a teenage son. "It's like being a musician or an artist; they sometimes just don't allow room for anything else to enter."

But his reticence goes deeper than time commitments. He saw his brother Dennis through a divorce, and witnessing the usual arguments and rocky patches of his siblings' marriages made him retreat further. "Harry can't understand friction," says Dennis.

While Harry's not afraid to go head on with risk in the sporting world, getting emotionally attached is another matter.

"Because of the notoriety I get from time to time, people come on really strong. The next thing you know, they're not any more sincere than anyone else," he says. "Real love starts to develop after you get going. When the right person comes along, I'll know it. I've never ruled marriage out, but I don't want to get hurt."

After earning his B.A. in recreation, Harry was aiming for a job teaching sports or running a recreational facility, but the job market still wasn't beckoning him. So he opted for still more school, overcoming his usual dread of academics. Education and employment weren't the only reasons Harry signed on for a master's degree in physical education. Cal State had a spanking new physical education facility, with two swimming pools and a basketball gymnasium.

"The new facility would be like a country club—an unusual reason for choosing to do a master's degree, but it was a good enough excuse for me," Harry says.

As the only blind student ever in the master's degree program, Harry was a laboratory for adaptive education, says Dick Rivenes, one of Harry's professors.

"He had a reputation as someone who wasn't sitting around waiting for life to happen. He was out there," Dick says. "He became a model for a lot of the things we talked about in classes. I learned things from him that I often used in adaptive education. People wouldn't just help Harry to a chair, for example, but would also try to take his weight, lift him, help him walk. It was as if he were not just blind, but helpless."

If anyone is responsible for turning Harry into a running zealot, it is Dick. Harry had tried jogging at City College with classmate Mike Megas. Their technique of running while holding Harry's cane between them prohibited any kind of arm swing. Their rhythm was stiff and awkward and slow, and Harry soon lost interest.

Then Dick convinced him to sign up for a class in weight training and conditioning that included a half-mile warm-up run. Dick wanted to develop a technique that would allow blind people to run in a free-body position. And for Harry—well, it was too good of a challenge to pass up.

Dick attached a key chain to his waist and ran about five yards ahead of Harry, who kept the sound of the jangling keys just ahead of him and to the left.

"He had a typical blind person's reaction to running— head back, very fearful of running into something, falling, or tripping," Dick says. But soon, he was running smoothly, if not terribly fast. He had a few nasty spills, but suffered nothing more than scraped knees and elbows.

The technique worked well enough, but Harry was more interested in swimming and diving in Cal State's new pool than in logging miles around a track. In fact, he says, he might never have pursued running if it hadn't been for a little sibling rivalry.

Harry's brother Peter had been jogging two miles a day as a way to lose weight when he decided to run the Bay-to-Breakers Race in San Francisco. Back then, the race little resembled the fest of revelry for tens of thousands of runners that it has become today. Harry went to watch Peter and 700 other runners complete the course from San Francisco's bay-side piers, through downtown and Golden Gate Park to Ocean Beach. Peter finished the seven-and three-quarter mile run in less than an hour, and pricked Harry's competitive streak. After all, at 6 feet and 160 pounds, Harry had much more of a runner's build than his brother, and had been working out with weights.

Harry told Rivenes how much he wanted to run the race. "Nobody seems to think I could do it without killing myself or getting somebody else hurt. Even my brother said that I could never make it through all those runners and the cars that cut in and out between them," Harry said.

"Nonsense," was Rivenes' response. "I'll run it with you."

Harry never looked back. His interest in running had been stirred up, and this time it would last and grow. "Grow?" says Harry. "'Explode' would be a more accurate description."

Chapter 4
WHAT'S THE WORD?
CONFIDENCE!

"The first competitive race we entered was a 10K on the track at Cal State Hayward. We went out there not knowing a thing, and ran the first mile in 6 minutes, 12 seconds and the second mile in 6:20. We were capable of running that pace, but not sustaining it. With about five or six laps to go, my mind kept going but my body gave out. I staggered off the track and collapsed onto the infield. Someone came out from the bleachers and escorted Harry to the end. It was pretty dramatic to watch: the blind guy finishes and the guide gets taken to the hospital."
—Bill Welch, Harry's running partner, 1968–1970.

Dick Rivenes knew how much Harry wanted to be a Bay-to-Breakers runner. He also knew what Harry's enthusiasm could do to his studies. For Harry, listening to textbook tapes, slogging through braille reading assignments, and writing papers was a drag, something that took away from his precious hours of swimming, diving, or weight lifting.

As a track and football coach, Dick could understand the lure of sports. As a professor—and the chairman of Harry's master's thesis committee—he also knew how important it was for Harry to reach his academic goals. So he cooked up a plan using running as a motivational carrot. He agreed to guide Harry in the race and train with him, but only after Harry had finished the research for his thesis.

Harry was pretty irritated by the idea. "I thought he was going to back out on me," he says. "How could I ever be a Bay-to-Breakers runner if I buried myself in library books?"

But Harry didn't have much choice. He finished his

research in March, two months before the race. Dick may have been hoping that Harry wouldn't live up to his end of the bargain. The coach was overweight, out of shape, and had never run in an organized race. But true to his word, he started training with Harry, exploring different techniques to keep them tethered together without sacrificing freedom of movement.

First they tried holding Harry's white cane between them, which was clumsy and stiff. A rope between them was more flexible, but Harry felt as if he were being dragged along by a leash. Using the jangling of keys seemed to work, until the noise of water sprinklers drowned out the sound and a disoriented Harry stumbled on a curb and took a spill.

Incredibly, the best method turned out to be simply bumping elbows as the two ran along side-by-side.

"It doesn't interfere with the sighted person, or with Harry," Dick says. "When we came to curbs, he would grab my elbow and we'd negotiate them together."

For Harry, it was exhilarating to be able to stretch out and, for the first time, really run. With each training run, the intense concentration on every stride and the fear of falling no longer crowded his mind.

"I was able to enjoy the scenery as it went by—the chirping of the birds and the rustling of the leaves on the trees," says Harry. "All of the plants and flowers around campus had their own special fragrances, and I always knew where I was when I ran past them."

Harry's guided running technique does attract attention. It's more subtle than the leash method most blind runners use—and it's hard to tell why two runners would want to move so closely in tandem. More than once, people have made crude comments at the sight of two men touching as they ran together.

"Once at St. Ignatius High School, there were these kids with their buddies trying to be cool. They called Harry and his partner 'faggots' and 'queers,'" Harry's sister, Joanne remembers. "Harry took his artificial eye out and said, 'Did you ever think I might be blind?' They just shut up."

Harry had been just a kid when he first saw the Bay-to-Breakers runners making their way to the finish line at Ocean Beach, a block away from his family's restaurant. Known then as the Cross City Race, the event had never attracted more than about 100 runners since its inception in 1912.

In the 1950s, running was still thought of as kind of a nutty thing to do. Why would anyone purposefully want to sweat and strain and make their heart pound as they loped along the city streets? But each year on a spring Sunday morning, Harry's father would telephone from the restaurant and say, "Come quick! The runners are coming in!"

Harry thought the whole thing was a fake or a publicity stunt. "Nobody could run all the way from the Ferry Building across the city to the beach," he remembers thinking. "There were hills and traffic. It was almost eight miles. It seemed impossible."

In the 1960s, as Harry's eyesight deteriorated, he no longer had any interest in watching the parade of runners straggle in each spring. But the race itself was just gaining momentum. The physical fitness craze was on. It was becoming a familiar sight to see people clad in shorts, T-shirts and athletic shoes jogging along the paths in Golden Gate Park.

The race was re-crowned with the catchy and appropriate title of Bay-to-Breakers in 1963. Since then the race has boomed in popularity and notoriety, becoming one of the best-loved and wackiest running extravaganzas in the country. The longest continuously run footrace in the world, Bay-to-Breakers now draws at least 80,000 participants each year, many dressed in zany costumes, pushing their kids in strollers, even clustered together in "centipede" formations.

In 1967, Bay-to-Breakers was still a glinting dream for Harry. When he saw his brother Peter finish the course, it was the last time he would be satisfied to go to the race as a spectator.

By race day 1968, Harry and Dick had trained for two

months. They had never run more than six miles in one stretch, but were hoping that determination would make up for lack of endurance.

The night before the race, Harry and his brother drove over the course, and realized that the route certainly was a fair representation of San Francisco's famous vertical terrain. The high point of the race was Hayes Street Hill, which rises about 300 feet in five short blocks.

"When we started up Hayes Street, the seat in the car tilted farther and farther back, and the car strained slightly as we approached the crest," Harry remembers. "It was a monster."

Harry didn't fret much about the hills, or the distance of the course. He was too worried about whether the race officials would let him run at all. Harry was the first blind man to enter Bay-to-Breakers, and he knew that to some people, his disability simply represented liability and an accident waiting to happen.

Indeed, early the next morning, when he and Dick walked into the YMCA to pick up their race numbers, Harry's white cane stopped conversations cold. "Everyone seemed to spread apart and make a wide path in front of me," he says. "It was amusing at first, as if I had the measles or some other contagious disease."

A doctor at the check-in table listened to Harry's heart and passed him through with no comment on his blindness. Harry took off his warm-up suit, pinned on his number and ditched his white cane.

"At that moment, everything changed. Now I was a runner, no longer just a blind man. As we walked around the gym and made our way outside, I found out for the first time what it was like to be just another athlete. Very few of the runners realized that I was being guided and no longer did they step aside and hush as I walked through."

The two stepped into the sunshine of the Embarcadero waterfront piers, and warmed up by jogging a few blocks to the starting line. Several runners saw Harry and Dick practicing, touching elbows as they ran over railroad tracks and road bumps, and offered greetings and words of encouragement.

"It was unlike anything I had ever experienced before. None of them knew me, yet they seemed so enthusiastic about me being there."

It was Harry's first taste of the camaraderie of athletics, and of being accepted not just as part of the sighted world, but also as a role model and inspiration.

A whistle blew in the front of the crowd, and the nervous chatter stopped in a moment of anticipation. Harry heard a runner say, "Get ready, the gun is up," and thought back on that memorable day ten years earlier at Don Pedro Lake. Once again it was a bright Sunday morning, and once again Harry was facing the unknown of physical challenge. But this time it was a wall of people in front of him, not a wall of water.

The gun fired. A cheer went up among the runners and the crowd lining the streets. Harry started off at a slow pace, holding on to his partner's arm as the runners spread out.

"Bring on that Hayes Street Hill," Harry yelled. "I'll eat it up."

"Save your energy," Dick advised. "You may need it a little later." As it turned out, he would be the one needing his advice.

For the first mile and a half, the two passed hundreds of slower runners. Then they turned a corner for a look at the Hayes Street Hill.

"Oh God, there it is," Dick said. The hill was a solid escalator of bodies as runners slowed to a crawl struggling up the steep incline. Dick and Harry jogged up the first two blocks, then slowed to a walk-jog as Dick kept his legs going by pushing with his hands on his knees. It was clear that the coach was tiring.

"It was almost like climbing a mountain," Harry remembers.

"I pooped out a little on that hill," Dick says, laughing. "I doubt there was anyone bigger than me in that race. With my weight, it was a big deal. And I was tremendously nervous about screwing up. I didn't want to let Harry down."

As they reached the crest, Harry and Dick joined in the cheers of runners relieved to have survived the crux of the race. But Harry knew the effort had been wearing on the coach—and they still had more than five miles to go. The two made sure to reap the rewards of their steep climb, plunging down the other side like a roller coaster out of control. They then headed up a gradual rise into the trees and grassy slopes of Golden Gate Park.

"Harry kept talking about how sweet the park smelled, about the sounds and the cheers of all the people watching," Dick says. "All I could think about was getting through the race. I was a football player and a heavyweight wrestler, certainly not a runner. It was a big challenge for me."

"I could see that Dick was working hard, and tried to encourage him," says Harry, whose idea of a pep talk was to turn the motivational tables on his coach and mentor.

"C'mon, let's go!" Harry prodded. "If I don't finish this thing, I won't accept my master's degree."

"Don't talk to me now," Dick gasped. "I can't answer you!"

Harry had to wait a few minutes while Dick stopped on the sidelines to catch his breath, but the two were soon back in the race and within earshot of the ocean breakers at the finish line.

"I was tired, but we made it through in just over an hour—a respectable time among joggers," Dick says. "It was a fabulous thing to experience. Harry was on a high the whole time."

Harry may have started the race feeling like just another runner, but his feat marked the beginning of a flurry of attention over his athletic endeavors. The day after the race, The *San Francisco Chronicle* ran a picture of the winner, and one of Harry.

"Harry was a pioneer in promoting the handicapped section of the race," Dick says. "He has always been outspoken in pushing for and, by his own example, living the life he believes in.

"One of his reasons for running was to show people it could be done. He sees himself as someone who can do things and inspire other people."

"Inspiring" is exactly the word Mike Jones uses to

describe the impact Harry has had on his life.

Mike, like Harry, lost his sight gradually. First his night vision went, as his retinas slowly deteriorated from a hereditary eye disease. Then he lost his peripheral vision, then his depth perception. Just before his central vision went in his early 20s, Mike could still see well enough to witness Harry's first triumphant finish in Bay-to-Breakers.

"It was one of those things you see that registers in your memory," says Mike, 43, who is now an elementary school teacher in Aptos, California.

Mike lost his sight a few years after seeing that race, while he was going to school in Germany. He'd always been a runner, but suddenly he became sedentary. "I wasn't getting any kind of exercise and my weight shot up 25 pounds," he remembers. "I was really down in the dumps, trying to adjust to being blind.

"I remembered that a blind guy had run Bay-to-Breakers and that got me going again. I realized I could not only run, but run competitively."

In the spirit of friendly rivalry, Mike decided to beat Harry at his own game. He tried Harry's running technique of rubbing elbows, but found it created too much friction. So Mike tried tying a thin cord to his partner's waist, and holding onto a knot with his hand, about two feet away. It worked! As long as Mike and his partner were well-matched in speed and stride, both ran free of constrictions. If one stumbled, Mike simply let go of the cord without pulling or being pulled to the ground.

"The first time I tried this in a marathon, it cut ten minutes off my time."

Mike now uses this technique all the time. He is consistently faster than Harry over shorter distances, averaging six to six-and-a-half minutes a mile, but he has yet to better Harry in a marathon. It isn't enough for Harry to be the better distance runner, however. True to his competitive nature, he has resorted to some pretty sneaky devices to keep Mike from crossing the finish line first in any race.

"I was going uphill ahead of Harry in one race, and he came up next to me and said that line from a MacDonald's ad: 'Two-all-beef-patties-special-sauce-lettuce-cheese-pickles-onions-on-a-sesame-seed-bun.' It got me laughing so hard, I totally lost my composure. It took me three or four miles to pass him again."

After the 1968 Bay-to-Breakers, Dick Rivenes, along with Harry's brother Peter, joked about finishing in the "never-again" category. They'd had enough of mob-style running up and down steep hills. Not Harry. He was already thinking about how to improve his time by at least five minutes the next year.

"When we started out we were both clumsy and out of shape," Dick says. "I was looking at running simply as a workout, but Harry knew he could do a lot more, and he had a body that could take him a lot further. Harry was ready for a partner who was a faster runner and a faster set of eyes."

Bill Welsh was an undergrad studying physical education at Cal State Hayward, when he was bitten by the bug of the blossoming running craze in the late 1960s.

"I fell in love with running, and was pretty compulsive about it. It was kind of a natural for Harry and me to become friends," says Bill, now a high-school P.E. teacher in Lake Tahoe.

"I had always trained with nothing in mind, but through knowing Harry, I started to set goals. We were both committed to improving our times."

Harry, in turn, was delighted to have a regular running partner—and Bill was reliable, rain or shine.

"I made a commitment to run with him, and I did it religiously," Bill remembers. "Sometimes I'd see him sitting by his locker waiting for me, and I might not have felt like running, but I knew he was waiting. We put in some big-time miles and ran at least a dozen road races together."

The two found a way of communicating that was not only efficient, but also a good morale booster. During the sometimes seemingly endless miles, one would ask the other, "What's the word?" If all was well, the reply simply was, "Confidence!"

It was a ritual that the two came up with after their

first race, when Bill collapsed from heat exhaustion during a 10,000-meter event at Cal State's track. It was a hot day in May, and by the third mile of the race, both were gasping in the 80-degree heat.

"We're going too fast. If we don't slow down, we'll never make it," Harry warned his partner.

"It's all right. Just keep going."

Bill's arm was cold and clammy to the touch, Harry remembers, and the two were running awkwardly. Harry lost contact with Bill and nearly ran off the track. His incessant questions received only monosyllabic, trance-like answers. It was obvious Bill was in trouble, but Harry didn't know what to do.

With a mile to go, a race official shouted for Bill to stop: "Number nine—off the course!"

Harry couldn't get Bill to respond. The next thing he knew, his partner had staggered off the track and collapsed in the infield, and another runner was guiding Harry to the finish line.

"I thought he was going to die right there," Harry remembers. "I knew that if Bill didn't recover, I would never enter another footrace again."

Fortunately, the situation wasn't as serious as Harry feared. After a few hours of cooling down his body temperature and drinking water and saline solutions at the hospital, Bill was back in form. He returned to school two days later, and headed straight for the track to run ten thousand meters—this time at a sensible pace. Bay-to-Breakers was only a week away, and Bill did not want to miss guiding Harry to his second finish in the race.

With Bill, Harry sliced more than 10 minutes off his first Bay-to-Breakers effort, crossing the finish line in 52 minutes. In 1970 the two teamed up again, finishing the race in just over 50 minutes. The two also started a Bay-to-Breakers legacy, wearing signs on their T-shirts that read, "I get my thrill on Hayes Street Hill."

The sign has stuck with Harry as a good-luck charm, and through the years, others runners have picked up on the slogan, chanting the words over and over as a mantra to get them over the hill.

"I don't really like steep hills any more than anyone else," Harry says. "But if I really am supposed to be getting my thrill, I figure I should at least look like I'm enjoying myself. So I always run a little harder during that part of the race."

Harry and Bill stopped running together in 1970, after Bill graduated from Cal State. Back surgery has made running a thing of the past for Bill, who stays in shape these days by bicycling and cross-country skiing around Lake Tahoe's alpine meadows and snow-capped peaks.

"A lot of us who got out there when the craze was first starting really abused our bodies, and are now having problems. It amazes me that people like Harry, who have run for 25 to 30 years, are continuing to do it. I don't know how his body holds up."

The typical aches and strains of intensive running seem to bypass Harry, whose body just keeps chugging out some 1,500 miles a year like a well-oiled machine. The biggest barrier for him is finding partners. Now that Harry's a well-known athlete, world-class sports stars like former pro-football player Jim Plunkett or New York Marathon winner Priscilla Welch regularly offer to guide him in races. The trick is to find partners who are willing to train regularly, logging the miles without the honor and excitement of running alongside Harry to the cheers of the crowds.

In 1969, Harry heard about a running club organized by Walter Stack, a man whose eccentric daily training routine had earned him the status of cult hero in San Francisco. Walt, then sixty years old, would get up with the sun, ride his three-speed bicycle over the hills to the marina, run about 15 miles, then plunge into the icy waters of the San Francisco Bay for what he called a refreshing swim. Then he'd head in for an eight-hour workday.

Walt brought together enough runners from the Dolphin Swimming Club and the South End Rowing Club to form a Bay-to-Breakers team, called the Dolphin South End Runners. The group started sponsoring informal

Sunday morning races, the "Scenic Runs of San Francisco." Harry often joined in the races, and also started running with some of the Dolphin members who met Wednesday evenings to run a five-mile loop around Lake Merced in San Francisco.

The Lake Merced group evolved into a family running club, who named themselves the Pamakids, after an Indian tribe that had once lived in the area. The name was a natural, since the group wanted to include Pa, Ma, and the kids.

Harry looked forward to the post-run pizza dinner every Wednesday, and was disappointed when the tradition petered out a few years ago. But one Pamakid event that has maintained its longevity over the years is the annual New Year's Eve run at Lake Merced.

By about 10 p.m. on December 31, runners are in the parking lot, stripping off warm-up suits in the winter chill. Harry finds a partner ready with a flashlight to guide them along the lakeside path. As midnight approaches, the runners race toward the boathouse for an informal celebration to ring in the new year.

"I am always amazed each year when I think about my mileage totals," says Harry. "I don't have a training schedule, or the luxury of saying, 'Tuesday I'm going to do speed work, and Wednesday I'm going to do hill running.' I run whatever I can, whenever I can, with whoever might be available to do whatever they feel like running that day.

"But when I realize that I must run every step with a partner to guide me, I feel very thankful and fortunate to have so many friends who are so willing to help me reach my goals."

Mary Boitano Blanchard remembers seeing Harry every Wednesday evening, leaning against the lake boathouse, waiting for the other Pamakids to show up. Mary is quite an athlete herself. As part of a hard-core running family, she ran her first Bay-to-Breakers at age four, and, incredibly, finished her first marathon at the age of six.

"I had a lot of energy. Instead of bouncing off the

walls, my parents used to run me," says the 29-year-old nurse, laughing. "I'm definitely an adrenaline addict. I think that's what Harry is, too."

Mary often ran alongside Harry during practice runs and at races, but she was too young to be his guide—it's hard to rub elbows with someone who is two feet taller. Mary's older brother Mike, however, once partnered Harry on a practice run.

"I ran him into a tree," he remembers. "At the start there was a lot of noise and everyone was crowded together and he went right into a tree at full speed. I said, 'Never again.'"

Mike and Mary and the other young Pamakids would combat the boredom of long runs by playing "Harry Cordellos."

"We'd close our eyes to see how it would feel running," Mary remembers. "The farthest we got was a mile. It was scary; you completely lost the sensation of where you were. You really have to trust the person you're with."

"It still puzzles me how Harry is able to cover any kind of distance, adapting to elevation changes and curbs. But he does it," Mike says.

Harry impressed the kids with a lot more than his running. He got wide-eyed appreciation for his intricate carnival set-up. And he taught Mary to swim and dive.

"He'd swim the length of a 50-foot pool underwater twice before coming up for air. The word 'amazing' doesn't describe Harry. He can do so many things, it's like he has eyes."

Sometimes with Harry, it's difficult to tell who is guiding whom. One of the most impressive experiences is to walk or ride or run with Harry as he describes the scenery. In San Francisco's Golden Gate Park, when it's dusk, Harry easily has the upper hand, relying on his memory of curves and rises in the path, smells, or sounds to keep oriented. Harry's partners will guide him around little obstacles in the path. Harry, meanwhile, will tell his partner where the heck they are.

Harry's sense of direction in a car is nothing less than astounding. As an information officer for BART, Harry memorized every nook and cranny of San Francisco and the East Bay. It's dizzying to drive around with him as he performs his human road map services.

During an interview with a writer for *The Runner* on the way home from a lecture, Harry peppered his comments with detailed directions through San Francisco's maze of streets.

"Harry," said writer Mark Osmun, "We took a right turn off... whatever that street was, then two lefts. We're coming down to this stoplight—back across the street we were on in the first place. Why is that?

"Oh," says Harry, "On one of those poles in the middle there, you should see a No Left Turn sign facing that street. We had to circle around to avoid that sign."

Mark drops Harry off at his house in Ocean Beach, then, as he starts to drive away, he hears Harry shout, "Hey, you're going the wrong way!"

Harry met Gunter Hemmersbach through Peter Mattei, another Dolphin runner. Gunter and Harry were a striking match physically. The two were the same height, same weight, same age, and they ran the same pace.

"People who saw us running said we were in total harmony, with the same stride length," says 54-year-old Gunter, whose gray hair and beard, hazel eyes, and German accent set him apart from Harry. "I just went side-by-side with him and he could tune in just by the way I was breathing or talking. I didn't even have to touch him."

The two ran marathons and longer distance races together. Towards the end of one 20-mile race in Sacramento, all the runners were strung out along a flat country road when a plush-looking luxury car came up behind them.

"The driver was continually blowing his horn, and wouldn't pass us," Gunter remembers. "I turned around and pointed my fingers to my eyes to indicate there was a blind runner beside me. I couldn't just go into a ditch and expect Harry to follow me. And there was no reason the car couldn't have gone around.

"The driver stayed right on us, honking away. I thought we were going to get run over," Harry says. "I asked Gunter what was going on. He was so mad he yelled a few choice words, then pulled at his shorts as though he was going to shine the guy. At the end of the race the police were waiting for us because the driver had accused Gunter of exposing himself. After hearing our side of the story, the police decided just to let it rest."

Running with Harry definitely has its exciting and entertaining moments, but that doesn't always make it a picnic being his partner.

"He can wear out his partners, that's for sure," says Gunter, who stopped running with Harry in the mid-1970s when he moved across the bay from San Francisco. "It's draining. You have to make sure that every step you do, you don't make any mistakes. You don't want to cause him to fall.

"Part of it also is his energy. He really likes to gab. Once in a while, especially in a marathon, when it comes to mile 20 and you're tiring, you just have to tell Harry, 'Shut up, or I'll run faster.' It's all in a good sense, though.

"His abilities were such an inspiration for me—they were always more than I could give him."

There's a lot of joking and rolling of the eyes when it comes to Harry's zealous vocal cords. For the many people who like to run in silence, concentrating on breathing and pace, Harry can be an exasperating companion.

"I ran with Harry so much and got to know him so well, that his handicap wasn't being blind," says Peter Mattei. "We were doing a 20-miler from Sacramento to Woodlands and he's out there in the country, saying, 'Gee, smell the wildflowers, listen to the birds.' I'd say, 'Shut up and run.' Then he'd tell me I was running too fast and to slow down so he could breathe. I'd slow down, and pretty soon he was at it again, blah-blah-blah, and I'd say, 'Shut up and run!'"

Peter tells of the time he and Harry were doing the two-and-a-half-mile swim in the Ironman Triathlon in Hawaii. All the rowing clubs had war canoes in the water, and everyone would yell for Harry. "He'd stop every 50 yards and wave and say, 'Aloooooooooooha!' I'd say, 'Shut up and swim!'"

"ABC Wide World of Sports" took pictures of Harry and Peter on a tandem during the cycling part of that race. "There I am, down in the front, pedaling away. And there's Harry, in the back, sitting up waving and talking to everybody."

"Harry thrives on the companionship of being able to talk," says Phil Paulson, who met Harry at a Dolphin Club race in 1970 and has been running and water-skiing with him every year since.

"He asks a lot of questions to get oriented. He's certainly not shy or bashful. He has to be aggressive, or he wouldn't get partners."

Most of Harry's training partners last a few years, then move on. Some relocate to other parts of the country or get married or start time-consuming jobs. But many also simply burn out on Harry's relentless enthusiasm.

"I think the term is overkill," says Harry's sister, Joanne. "He just doesn't know when to quit. If someone usually runs six miles with Harry and calls saying his wife just had a baby and he only wants to run three miles or not at all, Harry gets all pushed out of shape. He doesn't understand other people's responsibilities or needs sometimes."

"Harry's a very persistent person, which made him the champion he is. But it also caused me to drift away from him," says Mike Restani, who was Harry's partner for 11 years and guided him numerous times through a tortuous cross-country race called the Dipsea.

"I enjoyed it a lot of times, but it got to the point where I felt there was very little reward. I was getting up at 5:30 every morning, working 40 hours a week in a screw machine shop. Harry couldn't understand why I didn't want to get up early on a Saturday, my day off, and go run 20 miles. He was very appreciative in the beginning, but it became too much.

"Harry became a great athlete," says Mike, who still

keeps a bag stuffed full of articles about Harry's and his exploits. "But he had a lot of help."

Harry does grumble about the difficulty of finding training partners. And, at times, he sounds like someone with a chip on his shoulder, talking as though he's owed something and people aren't living up to the bargain.

But just as often, he swings 180-degrees in the other direction. He fully realizes that he'd be dead in the water—and on the racetrack and the ski slopes—without partners willing to give their time and energy to help him fulfill his dreams.

"No one in this world makes it alone," Harry told the audience at a recent motivational talk. "Behind every success that I've ever had there's always been one person or a group of people that have made it possible.

"What would I be without the people who do things with me?"

After that first Bay-to-Breakers in 1968, Harry rarely got to indulge in any kind of anonymity. Blind athletes, especially ones with Harry's staying power, speed, and diversity, are an awe-inspiring anomaly. Harry soon found that fame has its advantages. Besides the buzz of media attention, he started getting invitations to be a celebrity participant in races all over the country.

One of his favorites is the Charleston Distance Run in West Virginia. Harry ran the 15-mile road race the first time it was held in 1973, and has done it 18 times since then.

"He's a big hit. He's got a following here," says Danny Wells, sports editor for the *Charleston Gazette* and former co-director of the race. "At first the appeal is that he's blind. But then people meet him and hear about all his accomplishments and are even more impressed."

As a celebrity runner, Harry gets flown to Charleston and put up in a hotel there. Race organizers don't have to give him much special attention. He easily remembers his way around a hotel by counting the steps from the front desk to the elevator, then from the elevator to his room.

Harry doesn't go to Charleston just to run. He usually speaks to some of the service clubs in the area and at running clinics, and takes time to enjoy the festivities that are part of the week-long Stern Wheel Regatta.

"He'll ask a few questions about what's going on, then never forget. He'll know the color of the boats. It's amazing to me. He never comes across as being blind," says Danny. "When a mile-long swim was added to the activities, Harry added it to his list. Now he runs in the race, rests an hour, and jumps in the water."

The Charleston run gave Harry a chance to meet one of the world's legendary athletes, Olympic track star Jesse Owens, at a dinner honoring both of them. Harry still can't quite believe that his accomplishments have put him at the banquet table next to his heroes.

"In what other sport could just an average participant compete in the same event with world-class athletes and then sit down to a meal right along with them?" he asks.

Harry is now practically a fixture in races from southern California to the East Coast, but the only one he's returned to without fail every year is his first: Bay-to-Breakers.

The event can hardly be called a race anymore. Unless you're one of the top few hundred seeded runners, Bay-to-Breakers is more like a free-for-all party stretching the length of San Francisco.

"Every time I start out I wonder what I'm doing here. It's scary at times. There's the fear that if you go down, 80,000 people are going to come down on top of you. But it's a sentimental favorite, a landmark celebration of what running has done for me."

One of the first marks on Harry's calendar every year is the date in May for Bay-to-Breakers. In 1992, the day marked Harry's 25th anniversary of running the race. And it turned out to be one of those perfect San Francisco May days.

"It smelled beautiful out. The fresh air was blowing in from the ocean, and I could smell the spring flowers and the eucalyptus trees. It was warm, with just a wisp of fog in the park."

As Harry stood with his partner George Mitchell in the sea of humanity jamming the streets behind the starting line, he thought about all the people who had guided him through the crazy maze of Bay-to-Breakers over the years.

Harry got a taste of his own inspirational prowess in 1973, when he ran with Peter Strudwick. Peter had been born without feet, but regularly competed in marathons. The sight of a double amputee guiding a blind man—at quite a fast clip—was enough to make runners stop in their tracks in amazement.

"Peter's form was smooth and flowing," Harry remembers. "He bent his knees slightly to absorb most of the shock that people normally absorb with their feet."

Peter's endurance training as a marathoner gave him a clear edge over many of the other runners. As they started up the rise of Hayes Street Hill, he was able to maintain the same speed as on the flats.

"The only time he slowed down at all was to guide me around somebody who was blocking our path. We must have passed more than a thousand runners on the hill."

For his 12th Bay-to-Breakers, Harry paired up with Dr. Richard Abbott. A few months earlier Harry had relied on Dr. Abbott for something far more critical than a race guide. In an emergency operation, the doctor had removed Harry's infected right eye.

"He had assured me that I would be back to normal in no time at all, and sure enough, here we were planning to team up for my favorite race," Harry remembers.

When Dr. Abbott fretted about finding Harry in the mob scene at the starting line, Harry couldn't resist replying with his usual wit: "Don't worry," he told the doctor, "I'll keep an eye out for you."

In 1992, Harry finished the race in 57 minutes—almost 10 minutes off his best time. But these days, the event means far more to Harry than the ticking of a stopwatch.

"Bay-to-Breakers opened up the door to new confidence for me in the very beginning," he says. "I can't imagine what it would be like to be in San Francisco on race Sunday and not be a part of it."

At the finish line, with the ocean waves rolling in the background, did he take the time to savor the moment of his 25th Bay-to-Breakers success? Hardly. He gulped down his traditional cup of juice, grabbed his warm-up suit and hopped on a bus bound for San Mateo. It was bowling league day, and Harry wasn't about to be late to meet his teammates.

Chapter 5

SHARING THE GIFTS

*"You talk about courage; just walking down the street
has to take courage for a blind person. Harry has run into
poles and stairways, banged his head more than a few times.
He wasn't born with his nose looking like that. He came
home one day and told us that he'd walked right into an
open elevator shaft. If it hadn't been for some big guy
grabbing his wrist, he would have fallen fifty feet to the
subway platform. You think you'd ever go out of the house
again after that? I wouldn't. I'd just sit in a chair. Not
Harry. He goes full steam ahead."*
—Peter Cordellos

1968 was a watershed year for Harry. In the spring he
became a Bay-to-Breakers runner, and a few months later
he completed his master's degree in physical education.
Harry was proud of his academic accomplishments, but
he felt far more acceptance in the sports arena.

"I really began to live the day I became an athlete," he
says. "In the sports world, I was always thought of in
terms of what I could do, not in terms of my limitations."

Finding his niche in the professional world was more
difficult. After almost ten years of higher education, Harry
knew it was time to land a job, and he was more than
ready to put his knowledge and experience to work. The
problem was Harry's timing. By the 1970s, many careers
were opening up for those with physical disabilities. Federal
legislation made it illegal to discriminate against people
with disabilities in many fields, including law, medicine,
technology, and electronics. But Harry was aiming for a
job as a physical-education teacher or a recreation
instructor. It still seemed a little too far-fetched to have a

blind man teaching swimming and diving, or putting together a gymnasium training program.

Harry and many of his teachers had faith in his abilities. But just as many people thought Harry's goal was unrealistic. He didn't set out to be a maverick, but by not settling for an administrative job, he was bucking the stereotype once again.

"It's tough to get going and fight the prejudice of some people," says Harry's blind buddy Mike McAviney, a customer relations employee at IBM. "I've had employers say, 'Yeah, you have the skills, but what if you fall down the stairs? How are you going to get to work? How will you know where the bathroom is?'"

Some people have a tough time seeing beyond a person's disability, says McAviney, who has been turned down for jobs and housing because of his lack of sight.

"There's another blind person working in the same office. I'm 5'10", 135 pounds. He's 5'7" and very overweight. We look nothing alike, but people call us by each other's names. They see the cane, not us as individuals.

"It's those little things that we have to fight. That's something we have to accept. I've been out at a restaurant, and the waitress will ask my wife, 'What does he want to eat?' Or people will talk loud and slow, as though I must be stupid and deaf. I don't get bitter, I just try to explain. Some people are at ease in five minutes, others you can never get to feel comfortable around you."

Harry's style is to educate by example, and he spent more than five years after college trying to prove to prospective employers that he could handle a sports- and recreation-oriented job.

Harry earned his Red Cross certification in lifesaving in 1968, and helped his former professor Roy Burkhead teach a swim-training program for young teachers in San Francisco. Harry would crawl out on the 3-meter diving board and dazzle everyone doing flips and turns into the water.

"He would do back flips and cut-offs and all kinds of

unique dives," Roy says. "He didn't always land them, but those 500 kids would just go wild. Each year the word would pass on. We'd ask the students what they wanted to do on the last day, and they always said, 'We want Mr. Cordellos.'

"He would have made a terrific coach, because his sensitivity is so great."

Harry's skills made him a natural to teach some extension courses at Cal State Hayward in adaptive physical education. In one course, Harry taught techniques for prospective teachers to use with blind students in arts-and-crafts classes.

"All of the students learned to operate the power tools in the shop blindfolded," he says. "They learned by the same methods I had used at the orientation center. And, while most of them would not have power tools in their own classrooms, they left with a much different attitude towards blindness than they had the first day of class."

Harry loved his teaching assignments at Cal State, but it was far from a full-time or permanent position. He went to dozens of promising interviews, and endured just as many rejections.

"On one occasion, I applied for a job as the director of a health club at an apartment complex," he remembers. "I was told that only one other applicant and I had the right qualifications. Then I was told, quite frankly, that when it came down to choosing between a man with sight and one who was blind, they simply wanted one who could see."

Most of the time, Harry felt, prospective employers weren't so honest. "The list of excuses in denying me a job seemed endless: I lacked enough education or enough experience or I was the wrong sex. Really, they were refusing me because I was blind."

Discouragement and rejection had its impact on Harry. He felt humiliated telling people year after year that he was unemployed and on welfare. His attitude became bitter and negative; he figured he'd be refused for a job even before he sent out a resumé.

"Many times I had to listen to such comments as,

'He'll never get a job anywhere,' or 'If he'd worry as much about getting a job as he does about running, things might be different.'"

It's true, Harry admits, that he put more effort into sports than he did into finding a job. "And why not? The runners accepted me as I was right from the beginning. There were never any hang-ups about the fact that I was blind."

But Harry knew he couldn't make a living with just his feet. Finally, 16 years after the interview with the Department of Vocational Rehabilitation that led him to the orientation center, Harry took a good hard look at the evidence and changed his focus.

"I realized that people were still not quite ready to accept a totally blind person as a program director or instructor in normal physical activities and recreation. I finally decided that I would have to take a job in another field, even though it was difficult to imagine that I would ever be satisfied doing an office job."

For Harry, it was certainly a trade-off. With an office job, he would gain self-esteem, financial independence and stability, and a sense of community participation. But he would be that much further removed from the passions of his life: sports and the outdoors.

In October 1973, the new Bay Area Rapid Transit District offered Harry a position as a trainee. BART administrators had never hired a blind employee, and, like many employers, were hesitant and more than a little nervous about the idea.

It wasn't a terrific marriage from the start, although working at BART did appeal to Harry's mechanical bent. The transit system was then state-of-the-art, and he spent his three months as a trainee learning everything he could about the slick, efficient trains and the tube system that carried passengers from San Francisco under the bay to Berkeley and Oakland.

The major part of Harry's job was to answer the hundreds of phone calls a day from people wondering about cost and travel times between stations, and about how to transfer from BART to the metro bus system.

During his training period, he had to show that he could do the job as well as any sighted candidate, which meant finding a way for him to use the telephone switchboard. For those who can see, operating the equipment is simple. They just watch for a blinking light, and plug a cable into the line to answer the call.

For Harry, a blinking light wasn't much use. He figured that, once again, he wouldn't be offered a permanent job. Then a blind operator for the telephone company came to his rescue.

Ken Metz brought his light probe to BART to give Harry and his bosses a demonstration. The device was worn around the wrist, like a watch, and had a long plastic stem that extended forward like another finger. When the switchboard signal indicated that there was a call, Ken scanned the board with the plastic stem until he hit the area with the blinking light. A photosensor in the wristpiece transferred the light to sound, which Ken heard in his earphone. From there, it was simply a matter of plugging into the line.

When Ken finished his demonstration, there was no question of whether Harry could handle the job as well as any other candidate. In February 1974, he got his first paycheck as a full-time employee.

He was off welfare, out of the unemployment lines, and into the working—and sighted—world. Harry's job gave him the opportunity to use his communications skills and his astounding memory of the Bay Area's streets, stations, and train lines. He was proud that BART riders could depend on him for answers about the transportation system. His hard work quickly paid off. In 1974, he received the California Department of Rehabilitation's Rehabilitant of the Year Award.

With a well-paid job and athletic prowess, Harry became a bona fide success story. But in his heart, he still wasn't happy. Most of the day he was cooped up in an office below ground with no windows. Harry felt cut off from the clean, fresh air he loved so much.

"Much of what I told people during a typical day was a long stream of numbers," he says. "When I entered the office each day, I felt as though I was taking on a new identity. I wasn't the marathon runner or the water-skier or the swimmer. I was simply Operator Eight, plugged into a machine like a robot. I couldn't escape." Then with the help of one of his co-workers, Harry managed an unusual merger between work and sports.

Ray Miller, one of BART's train control center operators, was also a long-distance runner. During one afternoon break, Harry asked Ray what it would be like to drive a train through the 3.6-mile trans-bay tube from Oakland to San Francisco. Then Harry admitted that one of his secret ambitions was to run through the tube, along the bottom of the bay.

The underwater system has separate tubes for east- and west-bound trains. Connecting the two is a hallway known as the gallery. If a train breaks down in the tunnel, passengers can escape through the gallery rather than walking along the potentially deadly high-voltage rails.

While the tube was being built, workers traveled through it constantly on bicycles, golf carts, and on foot. Miller himself had already walked through the gallery several times doing inspections and maintenance.

"I think I can arrange a run through the tube," he told Harry. "In fact, we can go one step further. No one has done it round-trip yet."

On October 9, 1975, Harry and Ray slipped through an air shaft in the building, descended 70 feet of zigzagging stairs and entered the main door of the gallery on a quasi-legal inspection tour—"just at a faster pace than normal," Ray later told a running-magazine writer who had heard about the exploit.

The two were in a long, dim hallway, which leveled out at 130-feet below the bay. The air was dry and dusty. They started off cautiously, Ray constantly bumping elbows with Harry and describing everything along the route.

"The only noise besides our footsteps and the echo of our voices was the hum from the light tubes on the ceiling," Harry remembers.

The calm lasted only a few minutes. A train soon

whooshed by on the other side of the wall, shattering the silence with an unbelievable, 80-mile-per-hour roar. The air draft created by the speeding machine sucked the steel gallery doors against their frames, rocking them back and forth on their hinges.

"It scared the hell out of him," says Ray, who had forgotten to warn Harry about the impact of the trains.

"It was like the sound of a tornado, or a roller coaster filled with screaming teenagers," says Harry. "No sooner had I settled down from the first surprise when another train blasted through the other tube in the opposite direction. It was the busiest hour of the afternoon commute rush, and trains were going by every six minutes."

Ray and Harry finished their round-trip in 75 minutes and climbed the stairs back to street level, only to discover it had started raining and the steel gates at the tube entrance had been locked. They wriggled underneath, rolling through a mud puddle, and headed for the showers in the Oakland facility.

Two years later, Ray and Harry repeated their run along the bay-floor tube, completing the round trip in 67 minutes.

"The first time through I had to read off the mileage markers for him," Ray told the magazine writer. "But the second time he damned near described it all to me. Harry knows the tunnel perfectly now."

Harry wished he could share his passion for sports with more of his co-workers. Few of them had any interest in the fitness craze.

"They weren't down on me, but they weren't interested in the fact that I had run a marathon on Sunday," he says. "There was a lot of trashy gossip all of the time about who went out with whom. Because I didn't share in the office talk, I was kind of an outcast."

Harry's lack of interests in common with his colleagues escalated into open conflict over the issue of smoking. Smoke-free workplaces were hardly the trend in the 1970s, but Harry was highly allergic to the toxic residue from cigarettes, and lobbied loudly for designated smoking areas.

One March afternoon, after a few sniping run-ins with people in the office, Harry couldn't wait to get outside during his break. He left the office deep in thought, and started walking around the block.

A man called out to Harry, warning him about a truck blocking the sidewalk, and offering to assist him around it. Instead of waiting, Harry turned and walked toward the voice.

"Suddenly the world dropped out from beneath me," Harry remembers. "My feet hit a metal rung, then— nothing. I had fallen into an unguarded freight elevator.

"A large, strong hand grabbed my left wrist just as I reached out with my right hand and clung to the edge of the sidewalk with my fingertips. The man begged me to hang on tight, then pulled me to safety. I slumped out over the sidewalk. He noticed some blood on my arm, and took me into the building for first aid.

"I could tell he was upset, and tried to comfort him with a few lighthearted remarks about taking a giant step for mankind. Then I asked him how deep the hole was. He said, 'Oh God, I don't even want to think about it. The elevator was all the way down to the subway platform. You would have fallen at least 50 feet.'"

Harry never found out the name of the man who had pulled him practically from thin air. He was shaken to the core by his close call. If he had been just a few inches to either side, he would have been out of the man's reach.

"All I could do was thank God for saving me," he says. "I tried for several days to put the incident out of my mind, but was not too successful. I kept thinking, 'Why was I ever allowed to gain confidence and come so far in life, only to step on a defective freight elevator grid and fall through to within inches of my death?' I wondered why I had been saved—I felt there was a purpose, something for me to learn."

Just after the elevator scare, Harry ran into an old friend, Jim Battersby, who had been his boss during an internship stint at an Oakland youth recreation program. Harry was the guest speaker at a March of Dimes Walkathon awards dinner in Alameda, and Jim approached him.

"After dinner, I went up to him and said, 'Harry, do you remember me?' It had been seven or eight years, but he knew my voice right away.

"He told me he was working for BART, but wasn't really happy," says Jim, who now works in human resources at Lockheed in Sunnyvale, California. "I was really impressed with his presentation, and told him I thought I could get him some motivational speaking engagements. He just lit up at that idea. So we worked up a brochure and I started promoting Harry as kind of a sideline for both of us."

Harry's job at BART went smoothly until December of 1978. During his first four years on the job, free time meant activity outdoors. He continued to train on the weekends with the Pamakids and the Dolphin Runners and swimmers. He also started asking for time off work without pay to accept the growing number of invitations to running, skiing, and swimming events around the country and abroad. And he didn't hesitate to accept the sporadic offers to give motivational talks.

Harry's life was busy and productive. Yet he had the nagging feeling that he was missing something. But what? Harry got his answer in the guise of a medical emergency.

Harry had always hated cigarettes and smoke, ever since his stint scraping ashes off dishes at his father's Ocean Beach restaurant. It wasn't just a matter of aesthetic distaste. His eyes were highly sensitive to second-hand cigarette smoke, and they were beginning to ache almost constantly in his often smoky office. Harry, like many of the early proponents of non-smokers' rights, was in a tough spot. He didn't have enough support to succeed in organizing a smoke-free workplace, and he didn't want to quit his job just because of people smoking around him.

Just after Christmas in 1978, he developed an infection in his right eye, and treated it with drops and an eye patch. His biggest concern was that he'd miss out on all his planned activities, including a conference in Washington, D.C., the Ski for Light in Squaw Valley, California, cross-country skiing races in Wisconsin and Norway, and a marathon in San Diego.

On New Year's Eve he joined the Pamakid runners for their traditional midnight loop around Lake Merced. With each step, his right eye throbbed. But that didn't stop him from carrying out his second tradition for ringing in the new year: going for an early-morning water-ski ride around Aquatic Park in Berkeley. Harry patched his eye with plastic and waterproof tape, and avoided any wild maneuvers that would get his face wet.

But keeping his eye dry and protected wasn't enough; it had developed an infected ulcer. On January 2, Harry's ophthalmologist, Dr. Richard Abbott, took one look at his swollen eye and put him in the hospital with a prescription for injections of antibiotics and eye drops every hour.

Unfortunately, the infection was out of control. On January 12, Harry's right eye had to be removed. Recuperating from the operation took Harry out of commission for three weeks—an interminable amount of time for someone who is neither patient nor a good patient when it comes to putting his passion for athletics on hold.

Harry's sister, Joanne, took care of Harry at home for two weeks, washing and draining his eye. Then the minute Dr. Abbott gave him the green light to run, Harry was out the door. Joanne and the rest of his family urged him to put his energy into his job at BART, rather than into sports. But Harry was afraid that he might lose his left eye next.

"I didn't want to go back until they put a stop to the smoking," Harry says, his voice revealing bitterness at the memory. "I wasn't going back into that room to face the same situation. If they took your eye out like they did mine, I think you'd feel the same way."

Harsh as it may seem, the eye operation was an important turning point in Harry's life. Like the elevator scare, losing an eye was a wake-up call. And this time, Harry paid attention.

"God had given me these gifts for a reason, and this was God's way of telling me to take another path in life," he says.

When Harry talks about the gifts he's been given, he isn't just thinking about his athletic and mechanical abilities. He considers his blindness a gift. With clear and healthy eyes, Harry might have been athletic, spending his weekends jogging in the park and swimming. But he wouldn't have been an extraordinary athlete, one who inspires others to live up to their potential. His blindness gave him the motivation to accomplish feats above and beyond what most people consider possible. Harry has impact. His commitment to physical challenge changes lives.

"Harry talks a lot about his faith in God and his attitude towards life," says Grant Garl, who met Harry at a family summer camp in 1983, and has been one of his water-skiing buddies ever since. "He's really developed a relationship with God. He heard the message, 'Are you going to let your handicap control you, or are you going to control it?'"

Harry realized it was time to share his gifts, not just save them for his own leisure time and enjoyment. While recuperating from his operation, Harry made a decision to focus his life on sports and on motivating others through his athletic achievements. Putting his decision into action was just a matter of how and when.

He returned to his job four months after his operation. His co-workers continued to smoke, and Harry constantly battled minor infections in his left eye. He wasn't happy. But cigarettes weren't the only reason for his discomfiture. A full work-week just didn't give him enough time to pursue his athletic goals.

Harry began taking numerous leaves without pay. In 1981, he angered his supervisors by going to Florida for three weeks to water-ski at Cypress Gardens shows commemorating the Year of the Disabled. When he returned, he received an ultimatum. He could keep his job as long as he took no more time off for sports-related activities, or he would be fired. Harry knew he couldn't limit himself to being a weekend-warrior athlete with two weeks vacation a year. So he quit his job in 1982, intent on developing a full-time career as an athlete and motivational speaker.

"I was slowly becoming a mental case at BART," he says. "What I wanted to do was help myself and others. I'm not some superhuman, and like anyone else, if I don't keep active, I'll lose it. Doing athletics is my day's work. It adds fuel to my fire."

Harry had found his niche at last. But getting there was a difficult road that brought much criticism from family and friends. After all, his job had paid well, given him medical benefits and social credibility.

Some people saw Harry's decision as a giant step backwards. His teachers at the Oakland Orientation Center for the Blind had been proud when he landed a job at BART—their training had helped him compete against sighted candidates for the position. They wanted graduates to have a professional vocation. A career focusing on athletics was not what they had in mind.

"He was stuck almost entirely on the athletic and recreational things," says the center director, Allen Jenkins. "He was not balanced in the attention he paid overall. He stayed more like what you would expect of a high-school youngster."

Harry is impressively independent in getting around town—and around the country—on his own. But he isn't the breadwinner for a family. Nor does he have to manage a household. His sister Joanne does the cooking, cleaning, and washing. She helps read his mail. She drives him to the store and the bank.

"Sometimes Harry lives in a dream world," says Peter, the eldest brother. "He doesn't have to take care of anyone. He doesn't have any responsibilities.

"He was making 20 percent more than I was at his BART job. He wanted to be able to do his thing, which is great, and they didn't give him enough time to do his running. Harry thinks that what he's doing is the most impressive thing in the world. It *is* in his world. But he doesn't always understand that people have other priorities."

It's not that Harry's family isn't proud of his accomplishments. They simply don't consider motivational athletics a full-time vocation.

"We don't think of him as a professional athlete. He's a blind person who has gone far beyond what is expected or was thought possible for a blind person to do," says Joanne, who works full time in a bakery. "But, you know, his whole life is fun and games.

"Harry says he works eight hours a day, and I just have to laugh. I mean, what, he gets up, and I drive him to a restaurant on my day off to have breakfast with him. We come home. Harry will make a few phone calls. Then he'll get on a bus, go over to the 'Y,' swim some laps, work out, maybe meet a guy to go running, come home, eat dinner, then get on the phone and answer some tapes."

"We have a big joke around here," says Peter. "When Harry talks about retiring, we say, 'You have to get a job first.'"

Harry's younger brother Dennis sees the situation a bit differently. "Harry really likes going to grammar schools and talking to kids, telling them not to smoke and about the benefits of exercise," he says. "And he ties a lot of his own recreation into it. He's supposed to be working, not having fun. I wonder if that's what people resent. Harry enjoys life. He lives life."

Harry hasn't lost anything by being in athletics rather than pursuing a job as a lawyer or doctor, says his City College math teacher, Evelyn Kerkhof. Quite the contrary. "He can do so many things well, has so much energy and speaks well," she says. "It's a great thing that he has the health and strength to inspire others."

Harry agrees that critics might be envious of his lifestyle. "I'm in the limelight doing this and that. Maybe they feel they haven't been given the opportunity to accomplish as much," he reasons.

"I could have another office job, and look back and say, 'Yes, I remember water-skiing in 1965 or jumping off the 10-meter diving tower ten years ago.' But that doesn't carry much clout when it's in the past. Now is what matters.

"We all have disabilities, some are just more obvious than others. I want to show that health is possible whether you're over 50 or blind or missing an arm. It's a way of life."

Chapter 6

GOING THE DISTANCE

*"I was Harry's guide during the national blind
championships in 1986 when he set a record in the
10,000 meter race. He won every event that he entered,
and was up on the awards podium receiving nine or ten gold
medals. He took off the one he received for the 10k and put
it around my neck. It brought tears to my eyes."*
—Kent Holder, Harry's
running guide since 1984.

It's impressive enough to watch Harry maneuver around
town at a walking pace, using his white cane to ferret out
parked cars, light poles, open doors, and curbs. He's agile
and consummately mobile. To witness him running is
nothing less than amazing. His stride is smooth and
confident.

Take it a step further and imagine him running 26
miles at a time. Hours of non-stop trust in his feet and his
partner to get him across the finish line without stumbling
or hitting the wall of exhaustion. There he is, racing
along, his hand barely resting on his partner's forearm,
for more than three solid hours. It borders on the
unbelievable. But Harry just grins through the miles,
looking as though he loves every painful minute of it.

Harry didn't even know what a marathon was when
he first started running. He asked one of his Cal State
Hayward training partners what was the farthest distance
he had ever run at one shot.

Twenty-six miles and 385 yards was the answer—a
marathon. "How could anyone go that far without
stopping?" Harry remembers thinking as he jogged

alongside his partner. "Then I heard that some of them took four or five hours, staggering across the finish line almost unable to walk. Why would people want to put their bodies through so much strain and torture?"

Many of Harry's compadres in the Pamakids and the Dolphin Club were training for marathons. So, of course, it wasn't long before Harry caught the bug himself and began hankering after the big one. By 1970, it was no longer enough for Harry to be a runner, or even a pretty darn fast runner. Harry wanted a marathon in his logbook.

Harry had never run more than 12 miles at once, and he didn't quite know how to make the big leap to true distance running. Then he met Kenneth Cooper, M.D., a senior flight surgeon for the U.S. Air Force, who now heads a sports training and fitness research clinic in Texas.

One of Harry's early running partners, Bill Welsh, had told him about Dr. Cooper's first book, *Aerobics*. Harry had the book put on tape, and listened to it straight through. It was like manna from heaven, reinforcing everything Harry felt about athletics and physical fitness.

A few years later, Harry heard Dr. Cooper speak in San Francisco. He hung on every word, listening as Dr. Cooper showed slides illustrating the positive impact that aerobic activity has on health and attitude. Little did Harry imagine that one day pictures of him would be the finale of Dr. Cooper's lecture show.

For the moment, it was enough to have a few minutes to chat with Dr. Cooper and talk a little about sports. "If a marathon had been scheduled for the next morning, I probably could have finished it on motivation alone," Harry remembers.

Harry didn't have to wait too long to test out his new-found zeal. In fact, he barely had enough time to train for his first attempt at a 26-miler. The Golden Gate Marathon in San Francisco was just seven weeks away.

Harry found a reliable and enthusiastic training partner in Peter Mattei, a member of the Dolphin Club, and, at that time, long-distance running chairman for the Amateur Athletic Union. Peter and Harry ran three or four days a week through the winding tree-lined paths of Golden

Gate Park. For the race, he teamed up with Jack Bettencourt, another Dolphin Club runner and swimmer.

He thought about the race for days beforehand, and dreamt about it at night. He dreamt that he finished in the dark, long after everyone else went home. He dreamt that he and Jack got lost and were disqualified for straying from the official course. He dreamt that he and Jack overslept and arrived at the starting line to find that all the other runners were far ahead.

The day before the race, the mailman delivered confidence boosters that took care of Harry's nightmarish pre-race jitters. Dr. Cooper sent an autographed copy of his latest book. Bill Welsh sent a telegram that said it all: "Good luck partner, the word is 'confidence.'"

Race morning brought bright, spring weather, a little too warm for Harry's taste. Jack and Harry pinned on their racing numbers and hopped on the bus, heading for the race start across the bay in the picturesque hamlet of Tiburon. Fewer than 300 runners were entered in the race, but it was enough people to jam the narrow road that led out of town to the rolling hills overlooking the bay.

For the first mile, Jack and Harry ran arm in arm to keep from tripping over their competitors. By mile five, the runners had spread out and the excited chattering had lulled to the sounds of breathing and pounding feet. Harry kept track of his pace, noticing that, at eight minutes per mile, he and Jack were a bit slow. By the halfway mark, the two were in the flats of Mill Valley, running slowly in the baking sun. At the 20-mile mark the two were in Sausalito, facing a curvy, mile-long hill leading to the Golden Gate Bridge.

Harry's visions of sprinting across the bridge in a victory run were dimming quickly. He was hot and tired. The road up to the bridge was bumpy and the cars that zipped by the narrow race path were uncomfortably close.

"I had to run behind Jack with my hands on his elbows. It was terribly awkward, since I fish-tailed back and forth in a jerky motion," Harry remembers. "I fell against the guard rail, and fell into the dirt as the sharp metal scraped my legs. I got up, but it wasn't long before I scraped against another rail. This time I didn't go down."

Jack had done so much running with Harry that he almost forgot he was guiding a blind man. "He's an incredible athlete, and when you're around him so much, you begin to take his abilities for granted. If he stumbled, you'd think, 'C'mon, pick up your feet.'"

The two maneuvered through the narrow chute onto the deck of the bridge. Harry's legs felt like rubber; his running pace had slowed to the "marathon shuffle." But his spirits rose when he heard the cheers of friends who drove by with shouts of encouragement. Harry ran downhill through the San Francisco Presidio, knowing he had less than a mile to go. He smiled as he realized he would be writing to Dr. Cooper with the news that he hadn't just participated in a marathon, he had finished one, running the whole way.

"I see the Green!" Jack shouted, as the two passed the San Francisco Yacht Harbor on the way to the finish at the Marina Green.

Harry heard the noise of the crowd waiting to greet the racers, and suddenly his legs revived. The two runners summoned up a burst of energy that carried them across the finish in style. Their time of three hours, 50 minutes was slower than their goal, but Harry didn't care. He was a marathoner, and one of the first totally blind marathoners in the world.

Jack's wife, Beverly, met them at the finish line, along with Harry's family.

"I was amazed by Harry's determination. He came across the finish line with blood running down his legs from running into that guard rail," says Peter. "I thought Mother would faint when she saw that."

Harry went home to share his victory with his father, who was too ill to attend the race. "When I ran Bay-to-Breakers, he really busted the buttons off his shirt telling people," says Harry. "Then when I ran the marathon, came home and threw up from all the water I had drunk, he said, 'All right screwball, go do another one.' He only lived long enough to see me do the one marathon. But he was really proud of what I did."

For Harry, the bright glitter of success quickly overshadowed the memory of cramped muscles, heat exhaustion, and the constant internal struggle of willpower over pain.

"We hadn't even crossed the finish line before I was thinking of how to improve my training and get a better time in the next marathon."

Racing 26 miles and 385 yards quickly became his favorite event. He ran in Mill Valley and Petaluma, in Sacramento and Santa Rosa. If Harry could find a way to get there and a partner to run with, he would eagerly spend weeks training for a chance to go the distance.

A few months after the Golden Gate Marathon, Harry was on a bus heading for the Avenue of the Giants Marathon, a race that winds through northern California's spectacular redwood trees.

"If it's possible to run 26 miles and enjoy every step along the way, it has to be on that road," he says. "I'm in another world up there with those redwood trees. For almost the entire distance, the trees rise two to three hundred feet above the roadway. I can sense them. I can smell them and hear them rustling in the wind.

"There's one place where the foliage goes over the top like an arch. It is so closed in you can't even see the sky. I can hear the footsteps hitting the road and echoing 200 feet overhead."

Harry has paced around the base of some of the massive trees to get a more accurate sense of their enormity. And he delights in his partners' descriptions of the scenery.

"No matter who decides to run the race with me, my partner always seems to find something new and beautiful to tell me about along the way. One person gave me an image that is still vivid in my mind. He told me that the trees rise up on both sides of the road like great cathedral columns."

The Long Beach Marathon in southern California may not have a glamorous course laid out across the Golden Gate Bridge or lined with towering redwoods. Yet it's one of the most popular in the state, and high on Harry's list.

"They really know how to put on a first-class race," Harry says. "There are bands playing. The course is well-planned. The safety and comfort of the runners is a big priority. There are people on tandem bicycles riding alongside us as mobile aid stations."

Harry was invited to be a celebrity runner in the first Long Beach Marathon in 1982, and he hasn't missed a year since. Harry has also been invited every year to speak at the annual marathon expo.

"I don't think I've ever seen anybody in my life who likes to participate in sports the way Harry does. He's driven to excel," says Gordon Proctor, a member of the Long Beach Marathon Board of Directors.

"To be such a fine athlete as he is, without sight, flabbergasts me. Everything he does without sight, he does better than I do. The guy is really into living. He's my inspiration when I want to quit. I ask myself, 'What would Harry do?' I know he'd reach down and gut it out. He's my hero."

When Harry's on the course, spectators yell his name and runners seek him out to run alongside and chat.

"Everybody in Long Beach knows Harry," Gordon says. "It's tough to run a marathon in general, but to run one and not see really inspires people. He's so popular down here, if he wasn't asked back, people would rebel."

Firefighter Kent Holder's first meeting with Harry turned both of them into nervous wrecks. Just before the 1984 Long Beach Marathon, the race director had started calling local running clubs trying to find a guide for Harry, whose regular partner was injured at the last minute. One of those he called was Kent.

"I had never even talked to a blind person before," says Kent. "But I volunteered, as long as he didn't want to run at a faster pace than me. It turned out that Harry's goal was to break 3 hours and 20 minutes. My goal was exactly the same, coincidentally, so the race director selected me."

Kent arranged to get off-duty by 6 a.m., which would leave him plenty of time to get to the race start and meet

Harry. What he didn't bank on was an early morning blaze that kept him on the fire-fighting line until just before race time.

"It was 15 minutes until the start, and no one was there. Harry was very, very concerned," Kent says. "About five minutes before the race, I finally met Harry. I was terrified. I didn't know how to guide and he didn't know what kind of guide he was getting."

"He even smelled like a fire," Harry says, laughing.

The two jogged to Kent's car to leave their sweats, and got to the starting line with four minutes to spare.

"I had no idea what I was getting into," says Kent, who has guided Harry in numerous races since, including nine Long Beach Marathons. "He told me that my purpose as a guide was to get him through the marathon safely. Actually he was more interested in me telling him what I saw—what the band looked like, what the spectators are doing, what the other runners were wearing."

E　　S　　S　　A　　Y

"A PERSONAL RECORD IN CONFIDENCE AND RESPECT"
The Loeschhorn Running Club Newsletter, 1984
by Kent Holder

The gun sounded and the third annual Long Beach Marathon is under way. Our first mile is a slow 8:10, but it is so crowded that I am glad for the pace.

Our strides match and Harry's gentle grasp on my right forearm is not uncomfortable. Soon the crowd thins enough for us to hit our pace. I can feel Harry's confidence in me growing as we maneuver along. He follows my lead and my instructions precisely.

"Tell me what you see," he says. I start describing the hill ahead.

"No, no. What does the city look like? What is that hissing sound?"

"It's a fireboat, Harry. There must be a dozen streams of water shooting 150-feet into the air. It looks like a fountain. There are rainbows in the spray."

A mile away, I see the Queen Mary, standing tall in the morning light. I tell Harry about it.

"This is a big, decorated intersection, Harry! There is a rainbow of balloons arching over the street. There are high-school cheerleaders and people in clown suits. The people are four or five deep along the side of the road."

My words are overwhelmed by the crowd's roar. Many people recognize Harry.

"Way to go, No. 46! You're doing great!"

"You're looking good too. We love you, Long Beach!" Harry shouts back.

Harry is having fun, and I am beginning to have fun too. Many runners know him also. There are always shouts of Hello! or someone adjusting to our pace to chat a bit. The aid-station workers all know him too. They've all been instructed that he drinks water and to place the cup gently into his outstretched hand.

We pass a pretty girl. I describe her and she blushes.

"This is Harry Cordellos," I say to her, and the blush turns into a smile.

We pass a wheelchair racer. Harry loves to talk to them.

"Get Coca-Cola to sponsor you," he shouts. "It's the wheel thing!"

We pass the eight-mile mark in one hour exactly.

"Right on pace," he says.

I wonder if Harry will slow down. He looks strong and our rhythm is good. The temperature is staying cool. The slight tug on my forearm seems natural now. I wonder if the next two hours will seem so easy. I've never talked so much in a race.

The miles pass quickly. Running with Harry is giving me a new perspective on racing the marathon. It feels good. At 22 miles Harry starts to slow down a bit. The course is mostly long straight stretches now, and the other runners haven't been a distraction for some time. I'm glad of that, since I don't have to talk so much.

Mile 23: 2 hours and 53 minutes.

"We've got 27 minutes to do 3.2 miles. I hope we can make it," Harry says.

"I can do it," I tell him, and concentrate on my

Harry (right) in 1947, pictured with three of his siblings. Peter stands behind Nancy, Dennis, and Harry. Joanne was born later that year. *Credit: Cordellos Collection*

Harry, left, and Peter, right, are shown with their parents, Peter Sr. and Myrtle, in the front room of their San Francisco home. *Credit: Cordellos Collection.*

Harry, during his stint as campus photographer, took this photo of the George Washington High School 25th Anniversary Invitational Relays in 1961.
Credit: Cordellos Collection

Harry stands outside City College, San Francisco, in 1962.
Credit: Cordellos Collection

Harry makes his craftsmanship come alive, explaining the intricate details of his carnival scene on display at California State University, Hayward, in 1968.
Credit: Cordellos Collection

Buddy and Duke watch Harry practice his golf swing in 1970.
Credit: Cordellos Collection

Harry swimming with Pete Biannucci under the Golden Gate Bridge in 1971.
Credit: Cordellos Collection

Everyone dressed up for Dennis' 1971 wedding. Harry and his mother are seated in front of Dennis, Joanne, Peter and Nancy. *Credit: Cordellos Collection*

Harry at work as an information officer for Bay Area Rapid Transit, 1974. *Credit: Cordellos Collection*

Double-amputee Peter Strudwick and Harry compete in the 1974 Bay to Breakers race.
Credit: Cordellos Collection

Dr. Kenneth Cooper runs with Harry on the Aerobic Center's track in Dallas, 1975.
Credit: Cordellos Collection

Joe Lewis and Harry enjoy a dip in the fountain at Kapialani Park after completing the 1975 Honolulu Marathon.
Credit: Cordellos Collection

At the San Francisco Recreation Center for the Handicapped, Harry teaches a Red Cross Aquatic Safety class in 1977.
Credit: Cordellos Collection

Harry and Astronaut Bill Anders enjoy a ride in 1976. *Credit: Cordellos Collection*

Harry holds onto partner, Mike Restani as they run in front of the camera during the filming of *Survival Run,* in 1979.
Credit: Mike Restani Collection

Harry's discus throw won the gold in his age category at the June '88 U.S. Association of Blind Athletes competition.
Credit: Cordellos Collection

Harry and guide, Ben Thor-Larsen, cross the finish line in the 1989 Ski for Light event at Silverstar, British Columbia. *Credit: Cordellos Collection*

Harry learns rock climbing at CityRock Gym in 1992. *Credit: Carolyn Wells*

Harry prepares to dive from the 10-meter board at the University of Indiana at Indianapolis, 1988. *Credit: Cordellos Collection*

Harry competes for the World Trophy for the Disabled in Dearborn, Michigan, in 1991.
Credit: Cordellos Collection

Harry is at ease operating the drill press in his workshop.
Credit: Cordellos Collection

Harry runs with George Mitchell in the 1992, San Francisco Bay-to-Breakers Race. He hasn't missed running in the event since his first time in 1968.
Credit: Cordellos Collection

Harry and Kent Holder pass the 10-mile point in the 1992 Long Beach Marathon.
Credit: Kent Holder Collection

Harry on his "air chair" water ski, performing at Cypress Gardens, 1993.
Credit: Cordellos collection.

Harry (bottom, left) performing at the Cypress Gardens 50th Anniversary production grand finale, 1993. *Credit: Cordellos collection.*

Harry chauffeurs Ken Brockbank to the top of an eleven-thousand foot mountain on an ATV to teach a summer youth group at the Guru's Foundation retreat, 2000.
Credit: Rick Bennett.

Harry speaking at a youth conference held at the Guru's Foundation retreat, 2000.
Credit: Rick Bennett.

Harry leading a youth "trust walk" at the Guru's Foundation retreat, 2000. Half the young people are blindfolded, lead by the other half. Then they switch roles, after which Harry (top photo) helps them understand what they've just experienced. All of us need guides sometimes, all of us are guides, sometimes.
Credit: Ken Brockbank.

At the end of a youth "trust walk" at the Guru's Foundation retreat, 2000, Harry has no problem holding everyone's undivided attention. Because he has just taught them how to "see." He has also taught them that we're all in this together. Later that night, he will sweep the "weird talent show" competiton by playing *Take Me Out To The Ball Game* on his water-filled turkey baster. As he does in each of his motivational talks, Harry touches the heart of everyone with whom he comes into contact, and adopts them into his extended family.
Credit: Rick Bennett.

Harry doing some spring skiing with Bruce Sherman at Utah's Alta ski resort, 2000.
Credit: Anita Sherman.

Harry's Carnival just keeps on getting better, 1998. His mechanical miniature Christmas
Carnival is an annual tradition at the Stonestown Y.M.C.A. in San Francisco. Visitors look forward each year to seeing the carnival swing into action with authentic carousel music and the
atmosphere of a magic toyland coming to life right before their eyes.
Credit: Cordellos collection.

breathing. I won't allow myself to slow him down. This is Harry's race.

Mile 24: "I see the finish line, Harry! Can you hear the crowd?"

I remember how wonderful finish lines look in races and it occurs to me that Harry has never seen one. How will I find the words to describe it?

Mile 25: "You're looking great, Harry! Only two more 90-degree right turns and you're there."

We pass many runners who are walking now. We fly by 26 miles, and turn into the final straight.

"A hundred yards to go, Harry!"

My words get drowned out as the announcer sees us coming and says, "Here comes Harry Cordellos, the world's record holder for blind marathon runners."

The crowd roars, and Harry lets go of my arm for the first time in 3 hours, 18 minutes, and 55 seconds. With both arms held triumphantly over his head, Harry crosses the finish line. Harry has won his race. And I have set a new personal record in confidence and respect.

Harry and Kent team up annually for another southern California marathon, on Catalina Island. The rugged course, over steep hills and dirt trails, is quite a challenge for Harry—and for the person who is his eyes.

"It's one of the more difficult races in the West. To finish it is an accomplishment. To finish it without being able to see is simply amazing," says race director Michael Braunstein. "There isn't any other way to describe what he does out there.

"I think of Harry as a fixture in the race. He speaks at our awards ceremony each year, and gets quite a reaction from the athletes. He wants to compete and be treated like an athlete. He doesn't want the fact that he's blind to stand in his way. That's pretty inspirational."

Harry first ran the Catalina Marathon in 1987. He and Kent and Kent's wife, Ann, took the boat from Long Beach the day before and hiked to one of the beaches, where they camped with some of the other racers. It was

Harry's first time carrying a backpack.

"Harry handled the course like a pro," Kent wrote in his running log the day after the race. "I was pleased with the guiding, for he never fell or even stumbled. We ran nearly the entire course, only walking the dangerous, big downhill to Memorial Gardens.

"Needless to say, I had to be continually alert and vocal. I was exhausted, but not too sore except for my forearm, which is still swollen and quite tender to the touch where Harry's grasp nearly wore a hole in my skin. No complaints here. It's a small price to pay for the honor of being Harry's guide."

Harry finished the race that year in four hours and 49 minutes, far ahead of the dozens who took six to seven hours to straggle across the finish line.

"Harry can't change being blind, and rather than be depressed or worried, he makes the best of it. He's the first person to kid around about it," Kent says.

"We were running in a 10K in Catalina, the day after we had run the marathon. A lot of the people were spectators for both races, and someone asked Harry what he was doing out there again. He said, 'I didn't see the course yesterday, so I thought I'd come out here and get a look at it today.'"

Harry has finished more than 130 marathons over the years, clocking enough miles in those races to run from New York to San Francisco. He holds the national record for a totally blind marathoner, and travels all over the country to run 26 miles and 385 yards. Year after year he returns to his favorites: Long Beach, Catalina, San Francisco, Dallas–White Rock, the Marine Corps Marathon in Washington, D.C., and Avenue of the Giants.

But there is one race that remains at the top of the list, the one Harry calls the "granddaddy of marathons"—Boston.

Harry had barely finished his first marathon in 1970 when his running club friends began encouraging him to go for Boston in 1971. After all, his time in the Golden Gate Marathon had already qualified him with 10 minutes to spare. Harry's second marathon, through a freezing wind- and rainstorm in Petaluma, didn't go so well. He and his partner made it in just seconds under four hours. Then Harry heard that the qualifying time for Boston had been lowered to three hours, 30 minutes to contain the booming number of runners in the race.

"I wasn't even close," Harry says. "I had never realized how much I wanted to run in Boston until it got pushed out of my reach overnight."

Peter Mattei figured that, on a flat, fast course, Harry could cut a rather unbelievable 20 to 30 minutes off his time. He decided that Harry just needed a bit of pushing in training and on the race course.

Boston was in April. On a damp, foggy morning in March, Peter and Harry headed across the Golden Gate Bridge to Petaluma. Harry's first running partner, Mike Megas, brought his bike to the race to ride alongside and keep track of time. Gunter Hemmersbach joined the two as a support runner.

Harry was surrounded by strong athletes who weren't going to settle for anything less than 100 percent. They got it. As they crossed the finish line at Petaluma High School, they heard their time: three hours, 21 minutes, 31 seconds.

"You're on your way to Boston!" Peter shouted. "You've made it!"

The Dolphin South End Club held a fund-raising drive to sponsor Harry's trip. Within four weeks, he had an all-expenses paid trip to the 75th annual Boston Marathon, to run as a representative of the club.

Harry teamed up with masters division runner Larry Fox. The two were soon on an airplane filled with marathoners talking training, nutrition, injuries, vitamin supplements and, of course, running gossip.

"After being in the air for more than three hours, I still found it hard to believe that all of this was happening," Harry says. "After all, I had only been a runner for three years. And in a few days, I would be running in a race with some of the best marathoners in the world."

Boston was filled with runners: Harry met them in the

hotel lobby, on the streets, in the restaurants. The race is held on Patriot's Day, a Massachusetts holiday, and the only news in town was about the race, splashed cover-to-cover in the *Boston Globe.*

Larry read a feature story on blind runner Joe Pardo from New York, who had run the previous year and was back again. There was no mention of any other blind runners, but having some competition gave the race an added spin for Harry.

Harry took his usual pre-race tour of the course, making mental notes on mileage markers and asking Boston residents for directions to the finish line at the landmark Prudential Building. The two loaded up on carbohydrates, with the long-distance runner's favorite pre-race dinner of spaghetti.

By 6:30 the next morning, Harry and Larry had eaten breakfast and were on board the caravan of buses heading along the Massachusetts Turnpike to the race start in Hopkinton.

"It still didn't seem real," Harry remembers. "I was surrounded by runners from Texas, Oklahoma, Utah, Missouri, New York, Pennsylvania. I couldn't believe that so many people came from so far to join together for a race."

Just before noon, the mob of runners packed behind the starting ropes. Everyone was talking, nervously asking questions under the hot, midday sun. Harry vividly remembers the moment:

"Time seemed to stand still indefinitely. My stomach felt as if it had a hard lump in it. My throat was dry, and I could hear my heart pounding. I wasn't afraid of being hurt. But this was the big one. This was the Boston Marathon.

"I thanked God for the chance to be there, and thought of the whole gang of runners back on the West Coast who had made it all possible."

Harry reached into his pocket to touch his two good-luck coins. One was a penny given to him by six-year-old marathoner Maryetta Boitano. The other was a dime, engraved with the words, "Good Luck from the Pamakids."

Seconds later Harry heard the starting gun go off. The crowd jumped forward for a moment, but then nobody moved anywhere. There were too many people. Then they managed a slow jog, and within 10 or 15 yards, Harry and Larry were running.

Harry didn't need his partner to describe the scene to him; he could hear the raucous celebration going on all around.

"The spectators along the way were unbelievable," Harry remembers. "They had programs with the names and numbers of the runners, and called out encouragement as we went by. Even if they just yelled, 'Go San Francisco,' I felt the sudden spark of energy and ran a little harder.

"There were children along the way with orange slices and cups of water for the runners. We heard that many children went back to school the next morning bragging that they were the first to give a runner something to eat or drink along the way. Anyone who wore a racing number was a hero that day."

Harry and Larry settled into an easy, relaxed pace. Harry was glad that he wouldn't have to face any major hills until Heartbreak Hill at 18 miles. But then halfway through the race, Harry was jostled out of his silent reverie by a wave of enthusiastic cheering up ahead.

"You know what that is? We must be coming up to Wellesley College," Larry said. "It's supposed to be the noisiest crowd of all. All those co-eds will be out there waiting for us."

"Wow!" Harry replied as the noise got louder. "The whole student body must have turned out. It sounds like 10,000 people yelling."

"Hang on, Harry! It's going to be tight!"

The students crowded into the street, forming a chute for the runners about four feet wide. They yelled names, numbers, and anything else they could read on the T-shirts of runners going by.

"Come on, Joe! You're going great!" one of them yelled." You're halfway there!"

Harry felt a surge of adrenaline. He had passed Joe less than one mile into the race. Was that his competition coming up close behind? Or was it a case of mistaken identity?

The pace slowed down a bit. The two turned right at firehouse corner and slowed down even more as they faced the looming incline of Heartbreak Hill. Larry spotted his backup partner in the crowd and called to him to join in. Larry had been battling the flu all week and didn't want to leave Harry in the lurch at the last minute. Bill Cove, armed with a bottle of Gatorade, came up from behind and wedged in between the two. At the crest of the hill, Larry dropped out of sight.

"Congratulations," Harry heard coming from a loudspeaker. "You have just conquered Heartbreak Hill. You have less than five miles and it's all downhill from here."

Harry heard more cheers for Joe, and figured he was close at his heels, ready to pounce into the lead.

"I didn't even think that they might be mistaking me for Joe. I just wanted to get across that finish line ahead of him."

Harry asked Bill where they were, but no one seemed to know exactly how far it was to the finish. "Can you see a right turn up there anywhere?" Harry remembered the course from his drive through. His legs felt like two lead pipes and he was anxious to make it across the finish line before they turned to cement.

Bill pushed Harry to the right, into a tight turn. Harry knew they had made it—but no one could give them an accurate time. They funneled into the finish chute and listened for their time. They heard nothing except the wild cheers of spectators and runners.

The official time clock had been turned off at three hours and 30 minutes. It wasn't until after Harry had eaten his traditional bowl of beef stew in the Prudential Center cafeteria that he got hold of an unofficial time sheet. He had crossed the line in three hours, 30 minutes and 33 seconds. He never did find if or when Joe Pardo finished the race.

Harry whooped it up that night at a victory party for all the California runners. The celebration continued the next morning on the plane home, with champagne and cake for all the runners.

The 1971 Boston Marathon was history. And of course Harry was already thinking of the future, devising training techniques for the next year.

Harry ran the marathon in 1972 and 1973, starting and finishing the race with different partners once again. "I was beginning to feel like a Boston jinx," Harry says.

In 1974, Harry went to Boston with a P.R.—personal record—qualifying time of three hours, seven minutes. Jack Leydig, one of the Bay Area's top runners, offered to guide Harry in Boston. The weather was hot, then cool with a tailwind. The elements seemed right for Harry to get a new P.R. And this year, his partner was showing no signs of wearing out. In fact, Harry says, he could feel Jack's arm pulling ahead of him.

"Slow down," Harry said, "You're getting away from me."

But Jack knew Harry's limits.

Harry heard a voice on the sidelines yell, "Come on, Harry! All the way! You've got a P.R.!"

The two funneled into the chute and heard the official shout "3:06:16." Jack led Harry out of the chute to the Prudential Plaza, where John Butterfield was waiting. John had run the marathon in two hours and 30 minutes, then had run back up the course to cheer for Harry.

"What took you so long?" John joked. "Next year, I'm going to run this thing with you, and we're going to break the blind record!"

The three went to dangle their feet in the Prudential fountain, where the chilly water helped soothe aching, blistered feet. Of course Harry wasn't satisfied with just getting his feet wet. He jumped in the 45-degree water for a victory lap around the fountain.

John Butterfield had been stationed at Mare Island as a commander with the U.S. Navy in California when he joined the Dolphin Club.

"There was a picnic up on the Russian River and Harry and I did a three-mile fun run. Then we went out in the water. We were out in a canoe and he was diving off and swimming. He just delighted in any sort of challenge. Then he said he'd like to run with me sometime."

John was stationed overseas by the time he and Harry met up again at the Boston Marathon. He promised to return in 1975 to be his guide. Sure enough, on April 21, he was there to greet Harry as he stepped off the bus at the starting line.

The gun fired and John guided Harry out of the starting line at a breakneck pace. They clocked in at 32 minutes and 20 seconds for the first five miles.

"John, we're going 6:28 a mile. We've got to slow down or I'll never make it!" Harry gasped.

"Don't worry about the time. You're a lot stronger than you were before."

Harry was worried that he hadn't trained enough to live up to his friend's expectations of setting a blind marathon record. At least the weather was in his favor: Harry's teeth were chattering in the late morning chill.

"If it's cold and blowing and snowing, or rainy and muddy, it's not a problem," laughs John. "The only thing that will discourage Harry is if it's really hot."

John was amazed at Harry's memory of the course. "He was telling me things, even though I had run Boston a couple of times myself. I never paid attention to the fact that railroad tracks had crossed at nine miles."

John realized that he'd have to be vigilantly observant with Harry. "Situations that wouldn't even cause you to wince suddenly become serious. A crack in the road, a manhole cover, rough pavement, pebbles, rocks—Harry has to be mindful of situations like that. If you're going to be a good guide, you constantly have to tell him where things are—'move right, move left, pick up your feet'—so he lands very flat-footed."

Barking out commands is well-suited to John's military training, and Harry responds instantly to directions. John also turns the run into a narrative tour. He learns about statues and buildings that they'll pass in races, and talks about people he sees in the race.

"I'll say, 'Oh there's Bob Campbell, an Amateur Athletic

Union official from Boston. Let's say hello.' And Harry will give him a big 'Hurrah!'"

As the two approached the bottom of Heartbreak Hill in 1975, Harry knew he was within reach of running a sub-three-hour marathon. Once over the crest of the hill, Harry asked John if he could see the Prudential Building.

"You bet I can. It's getting closer every minute."

Harry's energy was beginning to flag, and his muscles were cramping. He told John he couldn't keep up the pace.

"Don't tell me you can't do it," his partner responded. "Do you think I came all the way from Iran to have you quit on me this close to the finish line?

"You're running beautifully. Of course it hurts, but that's what it's all about. Listen to the marching band up ahead, and stop thinking about it."

John admits that he pushes Harry. "He likes the challenge. I try to run the race to get the most out of Harry. He may argue a bit, but at the end he'll thank me."

With a few miles to go, John pointed out wheelchair racer Bob Hall, inciting Harry to catch up to him. John took Harry's arm and guided him smoothly around the wheelchair as Harry shouted encouragement.

"How much farther?" Harry panted. "Can you see the turn yet?"

"It's right up ahead. Don't slow down now, Harry. Bob Hall is right on your heels!"

Harry could hear the crowd cheering wildly for all the runners striving to break the three-hour mark. They made the final turn and ran all-out for the finish line. Harry couldn't hear his partner's feet hitting the pavement or even his shouts, above the roar of the crowd.

Harry and John were swept into the finish chute with a mob of runners. John recognized one of the Boston Athletic Association officials and yelled, "Time, time, what's the time?"

Harry held his breath. "2:57:42" was the answer.

"Now it was our turn to yell and cheer," Harry remembers. The scene was completely out of control.

Runners were laughing, crying, hugging each other, dancing around the crowded street. We'd all run Boston in less than three hours."

"You've made it! You've made it!" John yelled. Harry was the first blind American to run a sub-three-hour marathon. As far as he knows, his national record still holds.

Harry didn't have to tell John where to take him. The two headed for the Prudential fountain for a victory swim.

"It's one thing to compete in the Boston Marathon," says Harry. "But to run a personal best on that difficult and well-known course, and to establish any kind of record while doing it, is one of the fondest dreams of every long-distance runner. It never would have happened if John hadn't been there."

"It's as heartwarming as can be to be a member of the team with Harry," says John. "The Good Lord put Harry in my life. I enjoy his company, and he feels so good having a partner who takes an interest in him."

John, now a retired Navy captain, lives in Virginia with his family. He stays active in athletics and makes it a point to be Harry's partner in at least one distance race a year. The two are naturals for the Marine Corps Marathon in Washington, D.C., where Harry is an invited runner and often a guest speaker.

When Harry arrives at the Marine Headquarters in Virginia, his first stop is Henderson Hall for his traditional marine haircut. "He does it every year," John says. "It's a good-luck thing to get a real buzz cut by the Marines.

"I think Harry would have loved being a Marine. When he'd visit us at the Naval Academy at Annapolis, he was like a kid in a candy store with all the athletic facilities and midshipmen around who were always ready to be his partner."

Another racing tradition that started with John and the Marine Corps Marathon is singing. The two were running across the Rochambeau Bridge to the finish line in Virginia, when John noticed Harry's pace lagging.

"I started singing, 'Carry Me Back to Old Virginie,' and

he loved it. He immediately picked it up."

A runner next to them, obviously exhausted, also started humming the tune.

"The man later told me that we really revived him," says John. "He saw what Harry was doing as a blind runner and realized that his troubles were few. He couldn't thank us enough. Harry felt really good that he'd been able to help somebody else.

"Now it's a tradition to break into song as we're coming into Virginia from the Jefferson Memorial. We make up crazy words and try to outdo each other with funny lines. It lightens everything up."

In 1987, as soon as Harry's 99th marathon became history, he began thinking of where he should go to celebrate his 100th. Where else but Boston? The Boston Athletic Association agreed that it was quite an event, and invited Harry as one of the year's elite runners.

Harry asked Kent Holder to be his partner, and Kent jumped at the chance.

"I had been saving Boston so that my wife Ann and I could run it together. It was a dream I had nurtured for years," Kent wrote in his running journal. "Yet how could I refuse this once-in-a-lifetime opportunity to run with the national blind champion in his 100th marathon in the most prestigious marathon in the world?"

The two were flown to Boston, put up in a hotel and invited to receptions, banquets, and press conferences with the elite runners, including Joan Benoit Samuelson, Ed Eyestone, and Bill Rogers. The official race program featured Harry in an article—no one would mix him up with Joe Pardo that year. Harry was in a league of his own. "He was a hero of sorts," Kent says.

On race morning, he and Kent were allowed to warm up with the elite runners and start just behind them.

"It was by far Harry's best start in 11 marathons there. We were over the line in two seconds," says Kent.

Harry had run only one race over ten miles that year. His goal for this one was to win the blind division by coming in in under three hours and 30 minutes. Kent kept a lookout for other runners with guides, although it was hard to determine if they really were competition for Harry. The U.S. Association of Blind Athletes divides sight-impaired runners into three categories: B1 for the totally blind; B2 for those with very poor partial vision; and B3 for the legally blind, with good partial vision. B3 and B2 runners often don't have to run or train with a guide, which can make a tremendous difference.

"You see sparkling headlines, 'Blind Man Runs 2:25 Marathon,'" says Harry. "But the truth of the matter is that they're not all totally blind. It's a whole different ballgame when you run without any sight at all."

Harry won the division for totally blind runners that year, with a time of 3:25:43.

"I find it hard to put into words how satisfying it is for me to cross the finish line with Harry," Kent says. "People are crying and waving to us. It's a high that shakes your body from head to toe.

"He's given me something no one else could: a good look at myself. I knew I was capable of certain things athletically, but I attained new levels of self-confidence through Harry. And I learned what the word 'respect' means."

In 1992 Harry was selected as one of four Masters of the Marathon for the San Francisco Marathon.

"We wanted to honor the unsung heroes of long-distance running," says Mark Beal, who handled publicity for MasterCard, the sponsor of the race. "It was set up to recognize marathoners who have overcome some form of adversity and have gone on to inspire thousands of others."

Harry certainly fit that profile. He was chosen from a pool of more than 1,000 nominees, along with a priest from New Mexico who runs to benefit the poor of his parish, an Olympian who didn't start running until she was 35 years old, and a 70-year-old woman who competed in athletics for the first time at age 55 and who now holds the world record for the 10-mile race in her age group.

"These are four very special people," Beal says. "We were all amazed at Harry's zest for living each day to its fullest. We'd have to drive to do television and newspaper interviews, and even though he's blind, he'd be giving us directions. It's just remarkable."

Harry and his partner, Mike Etkins, were treated like royalty during the marathon weekend—eating at fancy restaurants and staying at hotels, even though he lives just a few miles across the city. On race morning, the two started off 15 minutes ahead of everyone else—something Harry lobbies hard for, since having to navigate through the squeeze of bodies and pounding feet at the starting line can be a frightening disadvantage without sight.

"This time I had three lanes of the Golden Gate Bridge all to myself with a police escort," he says.

"I've never felt so welcome in San Francisco as I did for this race. It's amazing how many pockets of spectators there were. North Beach really came alive. I was interviewed on television before I went to the starting line. Then I stopped at the top of Hayes Street Hill to be interviewed again. We lost about 30 seconds, but I was pooped anyway."

Harry finished the marathon in just under four hours—not his best time by a long shot, but he couldn't find partners to put in the training hours. Besides, he said, "Next week I'll be running in Charleston, so why kill myself now?"

At the age of 54, Harry still has that kid-like enthusiasm for going the distance—whatever his time. He'd like to get another sub-three-hour marathon for his log book, but he knows he'd need a rigorous training schedule: at least 50 miles a week, with three or four 20-milers in the last two months before the race.

Who knows? Maybe Boston will be the lucky charm again. Harry is planning a return to the 'granddaddy' of marathons in 1996, for the race's 100th anniversary.

"You always want to improve your times. I'm not the greatest blind runner there is—there is a blind runner from Germany who has gone faster," Harry says. "But I'll always have a piece of the record, being the first blind American runner to go under three hours. And if I help someone, if I inspire someone by running, that is more important."

Chapter 7

HEROES AND FRIENDS

*"Harry came up and introduced himself after a talk
I gave in San Francisco. He was so pleased and excited.
'Dr. Cooper,' he said, 'I believe in everything you say.
I recently ran 10 miles in 62 minutes.' I thought that
was good for a man 32 years old, but not unusual.
Then I realized that he was blind."*
—Dr. Kenneth H. Cooper,
Author and Director, Cooper Aerobics Center

Bill Bradley wasn't a sports star, a big-name actor, or a famous musician. He was a local television reporter in San Francisco—a young journalist just building a Bay Area following. He was also someone who profoundly affected Harry's life, without the two ever meeting.

After high school, Harry was in the grips of depression as he grappled with his failing eyesight. His family and friends didn't know what to do with him. He was isolated and bored. He tried to keep up with current events by reading the newspaper. When he could no longer read the print, he tried listening to television. But Harry found that TV news was even more demoralizing than thinking about his own life. It was at the height of the cold war. Russia was wielding superpower muscle, and America was in the throes of an isolationist, anti-communist frenzy.

"The world news was sickening," Harry remembers. "It seemed like every time I touched the knobs on the TV, we were being threatened with nuclear war."

Harry says he would have withdrawn completely, building a life around radio soap operas, if it hadn't been for Bill Bradley.

"He had a way of reporting the news that made me

want to listen rather than be afraid. He had a friendly way of talking to his listeners, rather than verbally throwing daggers at them.

"When we were down in the dumps, because of everything being bad, he could pull us out of it."

Harry tuned into the program every day, and looked up to the popular young reporter as a hero. In 1955, when he learned of Bradley's death in a car crash on San Francisco's steep Twin Peaks Hills, he was devastated. His lifeline to the outside world had been severed.

Fortunately, Harry soon found a way out of his isolated malaise. He enrolled at the Orientation Center for the Blind and discovered a world of possibility and challenge. He no longer needed to depend on someone else's perspective to pull him through the day. Bill Bradley and his compassionate optimism were tucked into a corner of Harry's mind— only to come forward again when he least expected it.

Years later, when Harry wasn't sure what major to choose at San Francisco City College, his teachers steered him towards journalism. It was a subject that seemed to play to Harry's strengths. He was a good writer, had endless curiosity and loved to talk to people.

"Journalism seemed like an interesting field. But I thought about how much I had disliked listening to those news programs years before. The politics, the crime, the threatening world events, it was all so negative.

"Then Bill Bradley popped into my head. I remembered that his stories weren't always about doom and gloom, and he seemed to enjoy what he was doing as much as I enjoyed water-skiing."

Harry signed up for journalism that first semester. By the time he was a senior, he was a staff photographer and reporter on the college newspaper.

"I liked Bill Bradley's approach of finding the human interest stories," Harry says. "Even in the midst of crime and war, there's always someone doing something positive and inspiring. I'd much rather focus on the good things. And if Bill Bradley could do it, I knew I could too."

Bill Bradley was one man Harry had admired from

afar. But now his own high-profile involvement in sports has given him the opportunity to meet many of the people who have inspired and motivated him: Harry had dinner with Olympian Jesse Owens; he sat next to Colombian running star Alviro Mejai, on the way home from a Boston marathon; he rode in a tandem bike race with astronaut Bill Anders; he ran with football star Jim Plunkett and Olympian Priscilla Welch.

Harry loves to tell of the time he met one of his heroes—who also happened to be a politician. When it comes to politics and politicians, Harry's opinions are vociferously critical. But this politician was different. U.S. Senator John Glenn was an astronaut first, the pilot of the Friendship 7 space capsule in 1962.

"I've always been interested in space flight, ever since the first satellite was launched," says Harry. "I remember sitting by the radio with the family day in and day out waiting for the Vanguard to go up. We held our breath during the final countdown."

Harry had even built a cardboard model of the Friendship 7 capsule, taking a series of pictures of it in simulated flight for a college photography project. His fascination with flight hasn't diminished over the years: One of his ambitions is to attend a shuttle launch at Cape Canaveral in Florida.

"Just hearing it take off would be exciting enough. Then to be part of the crowd in the gallery where people watch would be even better," he says. "There's a little motel where I stay when I go down there to water-ski at Cypress Gardens. Whenever there's a launch, everyone's just glued to the television. Right after it goes up, everyone races over to the window to see the vapor trail."

John knew what it would mean to Harry if he could meet Senator Glenn, one of the legendary heroes of the country's space program. After Harry ran the Marine Corps Marathon for the first time in 1978, John asked him to accompany him on some errands in Washington, never mentioning that they were heading to the Senate office building.

"I called the Senator's office at the last minute,

explained everything to them, and asked if there was any way to have Harry say hello to Senator Glenn," John says. "We went in and sat down in an outer area. I tried to keep talking so he wouldn't figure out where he was."

"I knew we were somewhere important," Harry remembers. "But every time the secretary answered the phone and said, 'Good afternoon, Senator Glenn's office,' I couldn't hear the 'Glenn' part because John would ask me a question about roller coasters or something to distract me."

"All of a sudden, Senator Glenn came out," John says. "I wish I had this on film. It was just beautiful. Harry was almost in tears."

"Are you really the John Glenn who went up in the space capsule?" Harry remembers asking. "He said, 'Yeah, I might have done that at one time.' He didn't seem too interested in talking about space flight. He was more intrigued by the fact that I could run 26 miles without seeing where I was going."

Senator Glenn took Harry into his office, and a five-minute hello turned into a 25-minute conversation.

"Harry was just thrilled, and the senator was amazed—Harry remembered more about Friendship 7 than he did," John says. "It was just a sweet moment in all of our lives."

When Harry first met Dr. Kenneth Cooper, he was in the throes of hero worship. He had practically memorized Dr. Cooper's book, *Aerobics*, and was thrilled that his lifestyle closely followed the guidelines set by one of the leading sports medicine experts in the world.

Harry attended a lecture given by Dr. Cooper in San Francisco in 1970, and hung on every word.

"It was one of the most amazing and motivating slide programs I had ever witnessed," Harry says. "He talked about the American lifestyle and what we could do for ourselves if we turned toward physical fitness.

"I sat and listened with pride and satisfaction, knowing that the Dolphin-South End Runners were a shining example of what he was talking about. I already knew we were on the right track. But hearing it from Dr. Cooper was a special thrill."

The next evening, Dolphin Club president Walt Stack asked Harry to present Dr. Cooper with a trophy that recognized him as an honorary member of the club. Harry was ecstatic.

"But I also felt inadequate for the job," he remembers. "Dr. Cooper had run the Boston Marathon twice. I had to talk about the tremendous achievement of running a marathon without ever having run one myself."

Dr. Cooper's achievements spurred Harry to action.

"During the last few miles of the Golden Gate Marathon, when I was tired and sore and cramped, I thought about Dr. Cooper and his message. It was enough to inspire me to run across the finish line, instead of walk."

Now it's a two-way street between Harry and Dr. Cooper. Their friendship has spanned 20 years, and they are each other's biggest fans.

"Harry's the most highly conditioned blind athlete in the world," Ken says.

Dr. Cooper's words aren't just heady praise for a friend. For 18 years, Harry has made an annual trip to the Cooper Aerobics Center in Dallas, where he undergoes a battery of fitness tests: He runs on a treadmill to determine lung capacity; he is weighed under water to determine his percentage of body fat; he has tests to measure cholesterol level, cardiovascular endurance, and strength; he is screened for cancer. It's a comprehensive examination conducted over two days.

"His level of fitness is vastly superior to that of most people his age," Cooper says. "He's off the scale."

A big part of Dr. Cooper's fitness regimen is about nutrition. Harry certainly pays attention to what he eats, but he's no purist. He gave up butter—unless it's served on hot garlic bread. But he still can't resist French fries, potato chips, and the occasional slice of apple pie à la mode.

"And you can find your way to my heart any day of the week with a good, juicy hamburger," he says, with a smile. Hardly the regimented fuel of dedicated athletes. Fortunately for Harry, genetics are on his side.

"He's very muscular and lean. His body fat content is the exact opposite of most blind people, because they are usually restricted physically," Ken says. "He's also intelligent and disciplined, which has enabled him to achieve world-class status as a blind athlete. If he weren't blind, he'd be right up there with other top athletes."

In 1991, Harry was compared to 4,976 men in the 50 to 59 age bracket. He was classified in the top two to three percent, with just under 13 percent body fat.

"That's high for him. In 1990, it was 10 percent. Twenty percent is normal," Ken says. "For most of us, our fitness level really drops off in our 50s, but Harry stays up there. He's in a category all by himself."

A few years ago, the clinic presented Harry with a treadmill to help him stay in shape when running partners are scarce. The clinic has adopted Harry as a sort of mascot—an excellent example of the benefits of consistent, vigorous exercise. Harry's a natural subject for the finale of Dr. Cooper's slide and lecture program.

"Pictures of Harry running a marathon are show stoppers. He proves it can be done. He's an achiever, a doer. He doesn't know what the word 'can't' means," Ken says. "He's just exceptional."

Chapter 8

THE ENDURANCE TEST

*"When I first saw Harry running around
Lake Merced with the Pamakids, I thought, 'Why would
a blind person run? Don't they make brooms?' I figured
that it would be no problem to beat him around the lake.
Then he pulled ahead of me two weeks in a row.
The next week, I was ahead of him, and just before
the finish, he yelled, 'Hey, stop!' I turned around
and he ran past me to the finish line."*
—Mike Restani,
Harry's running partner, 1977–1989.

When the starting gun fires for the annual Dipsea Race in Mill Valley, the place buzzes with a kind of outlaw excitement. It's as though the town sheriff just swaggered into the crowd, yelling, "Get outta town, you varmints," as he shoots his .38 into the air. Why else would 1,500 runners head for the rugged hills of Marin County, over precariously steep, rutted trails that are minefields of poison oak, brambles, and loose rock? This can't be by choice. These people must have been chased out of town.

That's certainly what Harry thought when he first heard about the Dipsea. His brother Peter told him all about it after running it in 1967, the same year he ran Bay-to-Breakers.

"After listening to his description of climbing over rocks, and tumbling and sliding down hills and ravines so steep that he was totally out of control and on the verge of disaster with every step, I thought these people were nuts," Harry remembers.

"Anyone who ran the Dipsea, in my opinion, had to be almost insane or else didn't really value their lives that much anymore. Listening to people talk about the cuts, the scrapes and bruises, and the broken arms and ankles convinced me that I would never make the same foolish mistake my brother had made."

Then again, the last time Harry had said never, he soon found himself on skis behind a powerboat, skimming into a whole new way of life.

Topped only by the Boston Marathon as the oldest footrace in America, the Dipsea Race began in 1904 when a small group of hikers from San Francisco's Olympic Club made a trip to the coast in Marin County and discovered the Dipsea Inn, a solitary hospice in the shadow of Mt. Tamalpais. The group named themselves the Dipsea Indians, and decided to hold a race between two of its stalwart members, Charlie Boas and Al Coney. The rules of the race were simple: Run from Mill Valley to the Dipsea Inn. The contestants could opt for the 11-mile winding road, or try to cut straight through the rugged hills. Boas won, turning the contest into a cross-country fest, and the Dipsea Indians knew they were onto a good idea. Since then, the race to the Dipsea has been open to anyone sturdy enough to withstand the course, a mere 7.1 miles from urban streets to the sea.

But the Dipsea isn't about distance. Or speed, or even strength. It's about survival.

The course begins innocently enough, in Mill Valley's Lytton Square, and follows pleasant, tree-lined residential streets to Old Mill Park. The pavement becomes dirt, then it's over a footbridge and up a rocky, rutted hill. Then the course really begins to strut its stuff. Around a bend to the right, runners face three flights of stairs—671 steps— up and up and up to the Flying Y Ranch.

At the ranch, runners have a short respite of smooth flat pavement on Panoramic Highway—and a quick chance to catch their breath and take in the sweeping views before heading down the Dipsea Trail to Muir Woods. Then it's down and down some more to a rickety footbridge and back onto a trail heading up to Hog Back Meadows. After the aptly named Cardiac Hill, the Dipsea

Trail—more like a chute at this point—tumbles back down through Steep Ravine, crosses a creek, heads up the last-gasp Insult Hill to the finish line at the ocean breakers of Stinson Beach.

The Dipsea Race is easily one of the most challenging and dangerous cross-country races in America. It's also one of the most popular. To minimize the impact on the sensitive coastal environment, the event has been limited to 1,500 runners since the early 1980s. The race invariably fills within a few days of registration opening.

When Harry joined the Dolphin runners and the Pamakids in the early 1970s, he began to think of the Dipsea in a different light. When race time rolled around every August, all he heard about was the Dipsea. The groups would hold practice runs, and discuss strategy and technique for getting through the precipice-like sections of the trail without injury. At the pizza parlor after Wednesday night runs, Harry heard all about Windy Gap, Suicide Hill, Steep Ravine, and Insult Hill. He also heard all about the head-ons and the near-misses—like the year one of the stronger runners slipped going down Suicide Hill and broke his arm in the fall.

He still thought his friends were nuts, but his curiosity was piqued—and he began to feel that he was missing out on something. One night over pizza, Harry brought up the idea of walking the Dipsea Trail, so he could at least say he had been there.

"I was shocked that not even one runner in the group felt I could do it, even walking," he remembers. "They had always been behind me in everything I had wanted to try. But not this time."

"I don't know how we could ever get you through Steep Ravine," Peter Mattei told him. "That place is really dangerous. One slip and you could go down 20 or 30 feet before you ever knew what happened."

"It was one race that people just figured was impossible for him," says Jack Bettencourt, Harry's first marathon partner. "He was left out of the Dipsea for many, many years."

Jack and Peter hated seeing Harry's disappointment, and tried to figure out a way to get him safely over the Dipsea course. On marathon training runs, Peter started guiding Harry away from the pavement of Golden Gate Park and onto the dirt roads and trails.

"It was mild compared to anything we would find over near Mill Valley, but we discovered that I could hike and climb, and even jog slowly over uneven surfaces," Harry says.

Jack had been a Dipsea runner numerous times, and figured that he and Harry should give it a shot. Even if they had to pick their way at a snail's pace, it would be a challenge and an experience for both of them. One evening, after a Lake Merced run, Jack casually asked Harry if he wanted to try the Dipsea Trail sometime.

"I know of some side paths we could take to get around some of the really bad areas of the trail. I think I can get you over," he said. Harry jumped at the chance. "Sure. Do you think we can run any of it? How long do you think it will take us?"

"Don't worry about all that," Jack said. "All we're trying to do is finish it. We'll probably walk most of the way."

Jack and Harry, along with Peter and another Dipsea veteran, Bill Zimmerman, met at the Mill Valley clock tower on a warm summer afternoon. The plan was to have Peter run some of the side trails and roads to determine which way would be the best for Harry, with Bill giving backup to Jack.

"Ready?" Jack asked. He pulled on a pair of leather gloves and gave Harry a pair to protect his hands in case he fell on the slippery trail. The group headed towards Old Mill Park at an easy run.

"What time is it?" Harry asked.

"Forget about the clock," Peter said. "Save your energy for the trail. The paved road isn't going to last much longer."

Harry figured that his friends—all competitors at heart—were keeping track of the time, but didn't want him to have any unrealistic expectations. Jack and Harry ran arm in arm around the park playground, then over the footbridge, which bounced and creaked with every step. Jack called out every bump, crack, and rock along the way.

"Get ready to climb," Jack said, as they stepped off the bridge and went around a turn. "There are the stairs."

They slowed down to a walk, as Jack guided Harry up a few concrete steps. Then came a long, long flight of wooden steps.

"We walk-jogged, alternating between taking one and two steps at a time," Harry remembers.

"We hit a road and jogged for a short distance, then got to another flight of stairs that twisted and turned, following the shape of the hill. There was another short stretch of road, then more stairs, up and up and up."

"Nice warm-up, eh?" Peter said at the top of the steps. "Now we're ready to begin the climb."

"Now?" gasped Harry. "I feel as if I've already run ten miles uphill."

There was no longer a road, just rocks and gravel and a rutted dirt path as the group passed the Flying Y Ranch.

"I could smell the horses and hay," Harry says. "It made such a difference to be away from all the smells and noise of the city. We were really out there in nature."

The group slowed to a walk again, negotiating a patch of thorny bushes that snagged their shirts and scratched their arms and legs. After another seemingly endless climb, Harry could hear the wind rustling the leaves of trees up ahead.

"That's Windy Gap, the top of the first hill," Jack said.

The four reached a clearing, then ran along the paved highway for a few yards before heading over the crest and down a steep embankment toward the Muir Woods parking lot. Peter, meanwhile, stuck to the road to see if Harry could save time on a longer but smoother course.

"Behind me!" Jack shouted, as the path narrowed abruptly and Harry started sliding on the loose gravel.

Harry gripped Jack's arms below his shoulders, positioning himself in what the two called their 'choo-choo train technique.' At times Jack's shoulders were almost as far down as Harry's knees.

"I learned why he was wearing leather gloves," says Harry. "As we slid down, he steadied himself by grabbing anything along the path—tree branches, plants, even poison oak."

The course became even more dicey, with precarious drop-offs every few feet. The path looked more like a water chute than a route meant for human travel.

"I heard a car driving through the parking lot at least 40 feet below, and knew this was the place where the runner had fallen and broken his arm the year before," Harry says. "Each time my feet slipped in the gravel, my heart leapt into my throat. But I tried not to let myself think about plummeting down the side of that hill."

Harry kept himself from pitching forward by sit-sliding onto the ledges and dropping feet-first to the next section.

"I can't believe people run this, even with sight," Harry told Jack.

"They know what they're doing, and, if they're lucky, they get through it without even a scrape," he responded.

Across the Muir Woods parking lot, Harry faced Dynamite Hill, which he says couldn't be any worse if it were a vertical wall. "At this point, my legs were about to give out."

And they weren't at the top yet. First came a long climb up Hog Back into the coastal forest, dense with ferns and cool, shady trees; then the final ascent up Cardiac Hill to the summit. All that remained then was a descent of 1,500 feet on treacherous paths strewn with loose gravel, roots, stumps, and the ubiquitous poison oak.

Jack and Harry moved into choo-choo formation for Steep Ravine. With Bill behind them, the three picked their way down, dropping off a ledge at the bottom of the chute. They crossed a narrow bridge and braced themselves for the final obstacle of the course: Insult Hill. Two hundred yards later, past the Dipsea hot-dog stand, they were cooling their feet in the breakers of Stinson Beach.

Harry had done the impossible. He had completed the Dipsea without falling once, and—Jack and Peter both checked their watches, shaking their heads in amazement—he had done it in 88 minutes, far faster than anyone had imagined possible.

"It's the toughest course I've ever done," Harry later told a writer from *Saga* magazine. "Your stomach jumps up to your throat. You have to run loose-footed because you never know what is coming up. It's like standing during a roller-coaster ride."

But, Harry remembers with a smile. "It didn't take long for Jack and me to decide to run the race for real."

"Once we worked the choo-choo technique out, it was a snap," Jack says. "All I had to do was issue commands: 'Get behind me,' 'Step down,' 'Step up,' 'Step over,' 'Hang on to my shoulders.' We just worked out a routine."

Fortunately for Harry, his partner was sturdy and sure-footed, since guiding Harry through the Dipsea was a far cry from the light elbow bumping of road races.

"His guide has to be someone he can really hold onto," Jack says. "It's not going to be a 135-pound runner, I'll tell you that."

The Dipsea Race was less than a month away. Harry ran the course in his mind over the next few weeks, visualizing places where he could run faster—or run at all—to cut his time. He and Jack did a second practice run, and then, a few days later, Harry woke up to the blast of Jack's truck horn breaking the early morning silence.

It was a typical summer morning in San Francisco— the cool fog settled in over the bay, shrouding the twin towers of the Golden Gate Bridge in damp, swirling mist. Jack and Harry crossed the bridge and turned off the highway just north of San Francisco into Mill Valley, where cars full of runners were backed up onto the narrow streets. The usually sleepy hamlet was wide awake, with a thousand-plus runners teeming around the plaza clock tower and spectators lining the streets.

Unlike most races, the Dipsea is a handicap event, with runners starting at separate intervals according to age and ability.

Race officials, amazed that a blind man would even be attempting the course, agreed that Harry would start with the first group to ensure maximum safety for himself and the other runners. He and Jack had already assessed the course for areas where they could easily get off the often narrow trail and allow faster runners to pass.

"We figured we could escape into the bushes or trees if people were piling up behind us," Harry says.

Harry and Jack stood in a roped area with the first group of 60 runners and waited for the starting gun to fire. Within minutes they were out of the plaza, running over the bumpy, paved road to Old Mill Park.

"It was just like in practice, except for all the other feet pounding around us," Harry remembers. "And Jack was pushing me much faster on the sections where there was decent footing."

Runners from later start groups soon began passing Harry, slapping him on the back and cheering him on.

"The other runners knew who Harry was," Jack remembers. "If there was a little crowding, they'd give him room, and they'd warn other racers, yelling as they passed, 'Take it easy, blind runner up ahead!' Everyone was so courteous."

The race-day crowds and excitement gave Harry and Jack an extra pump of adrenaline as the two fired up the hills, then sped down, jumping over rocks, roots, and vines.

"I couldn't tell if we were really running, or if we were just making a series of recoveries from a long, continuous fall," Harry says with a laugh. "As far as I was concerned we were flying."

Jack called out directions and warnings, and Harry braced himself for a fall at every step. But it never happened. They made it down Suicide Hill in a skiing position, a wild maneuver that elicited cheers from nearby runners. They made it up Hog Back and Cardiac Hill, then down and down the steep, bumpy trail to the Swoop Hollow Saddle. They joined the jam of runners pressing into the narrow Steep Ravine chute, then ducked off to the side as a pack of faster runners came through, bringing a shower of gravel and rocks behind them.

Harry and Jack slid and ran and tumbled down the

scree, then jumped the last three feet onto solid ground. Then it was only a matter of Insult Hill, a rutted pasture, a dried creek bed, and a few cow fences and thorn bushes to the finish.

The two pounded down the last stretch of the course hand-in-hand, and crossed the finish line to the raucous cheers of the crowd. Harry was the first blind person ever to run the Dipsea, and he did it in just over 80 minutes.

"It really was an accomplishment," Jack says. "I'd already run the Dipsea for years, but it was a challenge and a thrill to get Harry through it.

"People just thought it couldn't be done, and we did so well it was almost incredible. We beat over half the racers. Harry was so elated. When we got in, he couldn't wait to call his mother and tell her all about it."

Harry did wait long enough to finish the race with his traditional watery victory flourish, however.

"We've come seven miles. Let's go," Harry urged his partner.

Jack groaned. A plunge in the ocean was hardly an inviting prospect with the chilly, damp fog hanging low over Stinson Beach. But Harry wasn't about to miss his chance for a post-Dipsea dip in the sea. The two pulled off their shoes and ran into the breakers. Harry, with his penguin penchant for cold, found it a most refreshing way to scrub off the dirt and poison oak.

Conquering the Dipsea propelled Harry into the limelight. Numerous magazine and newspaper articles lauded the accomplishment as awe-inspiring, although more than a few people thought he was a little wacky.

"Harry's invited me to try the Dipsea a number of times," says Harry's blind friend, Mike Jones. "I admire him for it, but no way. That's crazy. That trail is hard enough to hike on. I like to have a fighting chance when I run."

Harry isn't alone, however, in mastering the Dipsea without sight.

"Harry inspired me to do it," says Michael Holmes, a 37-year-old blind runner who ran the Dipsea in 1985.

"Harry's motivated me to do a lot of things. I saw him on television back in the early 1980s, on 'Real People' and 'That's Incredible.' He could do all these amazing things."

Michael finally met his inspiration in 1983 at a U.S. Association of Blind Athletes meet in Missoula, Montana.

"Harry was the guy I always wanted to beat. In fact, everyone wanted to beat Harry. That was the goal. He's in his 50s now, and in the Masters Division, so it's a little different," Michael says. "But his nickname still is 'The Horse,' because he just keeps going and going and going. Sometimes you wonder where Harry gets his endurance."

Michael wasn't a runner until he became blind from congenital eye deterioration in 1978. Now he's a regular in everything from 400– to 15,000-meter races. Following Harry's lead, he mustered through the Dipsea with a friend from Illinois as his guide.

"I fell down a couple of times, but I'd like to do it again. It certainly was the most challenging course I've ever run."

As far as anyone knows, Harry and Michael are the only blind runners even to have attempted the Dipsea, not to mention finish it.

"It's a treacherous course," says Merv Regan, a race committee director. "There are some places where the trail is just wide enough to put one foot after the other. And some areas where there's a sheer drop down into a canyon stream. It's beautiful. It's a wonderful hike, but you've got to be crazy to run it.

"And you have to imagine if someone who's sighted is crazy to run it, these guys are certifiable."

Harry's on-the-edge feat in taming the Dipsea captured the imagination of local film producer Joaquin Padro, who, in the late 1970s, was trying to pull together a short film about running.

"When I first heard about Harry, I was very skeptical," the Spanish-born Joaquin said in an interview with *City Sports* magazine. "I had heard about this blind guy doing all these incredible things, and I thought someone was kidding me. Then I met him and my attitude totally changed."

The project's focus changed, as well, when Joaquin decided to build a film not just around running, but running blind.

"Most running movies are very artificial. They may look pretty, but the viewer doesn't get involved emotionally," Joaquin said. "We wanted to grab people with this movie."

Harry was planning to run the 1978 Dipsea with Mike Restani, a brawny, muscular, and dedicated Dolphin runner. Joaquin took a look at the two of them and knew he had the perfect vehicle for an inspirational movie: Harry and Mike, sweaty, grimy, and gutting it out over the tortuous Dipsea course.

Joaquin took almost three years, and spent $50,000 to make his 12-minute film, *Survival Run*. In 1978, a helicopter hovered above hills and gullies of the Dipsea, capturing the race from the air. The following year, with Harry and Mike running together again, seven cameras were stationed along the course to catch the ground action. Later that year, Harry, Mike, and some running extras were rounded up to re-stage portions of the race for fill-in footage. It took four months to edit 20,000 feet of film down to 450 feet of non-stop action.

Harry encapsulates the film's theme in the first frame, his voice narrating over a shot of him walking down the street in Mill Valley on the way to the race: "The Dipsea Run is like life," he says. "You don't run it, you survive it."

Survival Run was released in 1979, and won numerous film festival awards in the U.S. and abroad. Harry and Mike became mini-celebrities, and people still remember Harry as "the blind guy who runs that crazy race in the hills." The film is the show stopper in Harry's motivational lectures. Audiences never fail to exclaim in awe as they watch him, clad in elbow and knee pads, follow Mike's commands to run and slide up and down, around and over.

For many people who see *Survival Run*, Mike is the real hero of the movie, leading the indomitable Harry over the famous rocky trails, across the flanks of looming Mt. Tam, under trees, around bushes. For the Dipsea, Mike is more than Harry's eyes. He's navigator and stabilizer, breathlessly calling out directions and warnings as Harry hangs on to his arms, trusting his partner to negotiate the bumpy ride.

Mike and Harry started out as rivals before they ever met. Both ran with the Pamakids on Wednesday evenings around Lake Merced. Harry first impressed Mike by beating him to the finish; Mike couldn't quite believe that the blind guy was leaving him in the dust with regularity.

Then Mike saw Harry on the back of the Wheaties box and in *Newsweek* magazine, and realized that he wasn't pitting himself against just any runner. When Mike attended a Bay-to-Breakers sports seminar in 1977 with Harry as a featured speaker, he decided it was time to introduce himself.

"I wanted to shake his hand," Mike remembers. "I put it out there, and of course, he couldn't see it to shake it. I was pretty embarrassed."

Mike hung around and heard Harry tell a group of runners that he was trying to line up a partner for the San Francisco marathon in a few weeks. Mike jumped at the chance.

"I wanted to run a marathon, and I thought I'd run with him to pick up a few tips. That was in June 1977, and we didn't stop until 1989."

The two lived just a few miles from each other on either side of Golden Gate Park, a perfect meeting place for training runs.

"We discovered a lot of common interests besides running," Mike says. "We were both roller-coaster freaks, for one. And Harry is really intrigued by the Loch Ness monster. There was a documentary on television about it, and Harry wanted to know everything. I was his eyes, describing the world to him. He doesn't just want to know where he is, he's memorizing every bit of information to use for a lifetime."

The two trained together at least three times a week, then ran races on the weekends.

"I could hardly wait to leave work and go run with him. He's a lot of fun to run with, and I was getting in shape fast," Mike says. "When you have two people focusing on the same goal, it's hard to stop the momentum."

Then came the Dipsea and *Survival Run.* "We really ran our butts off for that movie. We'd run 11 hours at a stretch on some days, and it's a tough course. It was really exhausting," Mike remembers.

"But it was great to be a part of the film. It has inspired a lot of people, and that's something Harry and I will have forever."

Harry didn't stop with the Dipsea. He was just catching his breath after his first Dipsea race when Rudy Stadlberger, a world champion handball player, stepped out of the crowd at the finish line and asked Harry to be his partner for the Double Dipsea, two weeks later.

"You have to be twice as Dipsea to run that one," Harry joked to his audience at a lecture in San Francisco. Harry thought it sounded like twice the fun. He has run it seven times, clocking three hours and five minutes as his best time.

"The weekend after Thanksgiving they have the Quadruple Dipsea. And there's an ultra-running group that actually had a race called Dipsea 'Til You Drop. People have run that seven-mile course nine times before they finally roll over and say, 'No more.'"

Harry may not be nutty enough to try to Dipsea 'til he drops (although there's no telling if he found a willing partner), but he certainly has made excursions into the ultra-running scene, completing 50-mile races in San Francisco and Hawaii.

"Marathons had always been tremendously challenging," Harry says. "But the times I have finished feeling strong, I wondered what it would have been like to keep on running."

Running ultra-races requires a different strategy for Harry. First there's the training hurdle—finding partners to run at least 50 miles a week. Then there's finding partners for the race itself. It's tough to get a partner to run the same pace for an entire long-distance race.

"People get tired at different times and want to stop and rest. You're only as strong as the weakest link in the chain. If my partner is at a strong point when I'm feeling weak, then I'm holding someone back," he says. "It's a challenge with a whole different strategy and pace."

In San Francisco, the course went around the Polo Field bicycle track 75 times. "We'd run for an hour in one direction, then run around a pylon and change direction, so we wouldn't always be turning the same way. I got leg cramps and had to race walk the last six miles. It was pretty tough."

When Harry ran the Honolulu Primo Fifty in 1977, he didn't wear out nearly as fast as his partners.

Taking off at 11 p.m., he began running the four-mile loop course with race coordinator Joe Lewis, who could only go a short distance because of an injury. Lewis grabbed a friend to take his place, who soon quit as well, enlisting another friend. It was a slapstick scene of guide roulette, until Harry crossed the finish line eight hours later with his seventh partner. "I felt like a human relay baton," he says.

Another feather in Harry's cap is the Ironman Triathlon, the pinnacle event of ultra-athletics. With Peter Mattei as his partner, Harry became the first totally blind man to compete in the race, which entails swimming 2.4 miles in the balmy ocean off the Big Island, then bicycling 112 miles and running a marathon in the tropical Hawaiian humidity.

"I really enjoyed it," Harry says. "But I had only trained 26 miles a week, and got in maybe four training swims and four short bike rides with Peter before the race. So we took it really easy."

Harry and Peter finished in 16 hours, 26 minutes, a time which Harry is quick to point out includes mandatory stops to check for dehydration and 20-minute breaks between events.

"Then there were several stops for foot and back massages along the way," he says. "It was fun, more like a social event for me. As far as the running is concerned, it's just a marathon. It was a challenge to last that long on a bike and in the water, but I never really got exhausted once. I know with training we could knock off three hours without even trying."

Chapter 9

THRILL SEEKER

*"Wherever Harry goes, he's looking for two things:
a running partner and a roller coaster. He was with my
family for five days traveling across Florida, and we must
have ridden every roller coaster from Tampa Bay to Orlando.
He went 10 consecutive times on the Orleans Orbit at Great
America. I went on it once and almost lost all my cookies."*
—Jim Battersby

If there's ever a call for a travelogue of roller coasters,
Harry would be the perfect Siskel & Ebert of the stomach-
dropping, white-knuckle world of thrill rides.

He's gone upside down, over the edge, and around the
hairpin in roller coasters from Los Angeles to New York.
He's given the thumbs up to rides in Texas, Florida, Utah,
Illinois, California, even Australia. He talks wistfully about
coasters he has yet to experience: the Great American
Scream Machine in Atlanta; The Cyclone on Coney Island;
The Thunderbolt in Pittsburgh; the Rebel Yell in Virginia;
The Beast in Cincinnati. While Harry may get too tired to
run or water-ski or bicycle all day, he never seems to get
enough roller-coaster rides.

"It gives him more satisfaction than anything, as long
as he can run and swim between rides," says John
Butterfield, who has been Harry's amusement park partner
after every Marine Corps Marathon in Washington, D.C.
"He just loves the thrill of being upside down and turned
around. He's got a strong stomach, and he doesn't know
the meaning of being scared."

Riding a roller coaster is more than just a thrill to
Harry. It's one of the few times when being blind doesn't
make a difference.

"That's what's so neat about it," he says, revealing his kid-like delight with a big, dimpled smile.

"Blindness doesn't take anything away from the experience. You know when you're way up there in space and there's nothing around you, and you know where you're going when it comes down. Besides, most people are too scared to keep their eyes open, so they're in the same boat I'm in."

Harry wasn't always such a connoisseur of the topsy-turvy. As a kid, he could see the wooden peaks of the Playland- at-the-Beach roller coaster from his window. He loved watching the Big Dipper cars clack up the steep tracks, then plummet down the other side. But Harry was strictly a spectator. The thought of riding the thing left him ashen-faced and quaking.

"I never knew why people screamed and yelled on those rides," he remembers. "They'd be hanging upside down in some kind of cage and screaming. I thought, 'Why do they do that?' And then they'd get off the ride, turn around and go on something that was even worse."

Harry's mom used to ask him to go on the merry-go-round with her. But even that wasn't tame enough for Harry.

"I was about three years old, and I remember sitting in one of those big chariot-type things, seeing these big, black leather cushions all around us and the animals moving up and down. I knew they were only mechanical, but the noise must have terrified me.

"My mother loved to take us. But I'd always sit on the bench and watch."

Of course, Harry wasn't content on the sidelines forever. When he was a teenager, he saw a Cinerama show that featured the Big Dipper on a giant screen.

"My cousin told me that the movie made you feel like you were really on it. I thought it would be fun to see what it was like without having to actually ride it. It was so realistic. From that moment on I was really curious about the Big Dipper, and kept trying to convince myself to go on it."

The man who put the Big Dipper through its daily paces lived next door to Harry. Bill Smith, who also helped build the legendary ride, gave Harry an open invitation to test it out for himself.

"He told me that he walked the tracks every morning. 'Anytime you want to ride the Big Dipper, you come down,' he said. 'I'll put you in the front seat, I'll set the brake, jump in, and we'll ride it together.' I kept making excuses—that it was too cold, or too windy. I wanted to do it, but I was afraid."

One day Bill came into the family restaurant with a long, solemn face. He told Harry that the city had condemned the Big Dipper because the amusement park was built on shifting beach sand. The ride was to be shut down that very day. He had missed his chance.

"Right then I decided if I ever went to the Santa Cruz Beach Boardwalk, the first thing I was going to do was try the roller coaster."

Soon enough, Harry had an opportunity to test his new-found courage on a family trip to the boardwalk. By this time, Harry was at ease on the Ferris wheel, and thought the merry-go-round was for sissies. He and his older sister Nancy had even braved the Rock-o-Plane on top of the Emporium at Stonestown shopping center.

"It was a heck of a lot of fun. We could turn completely upside down," Harry remembers. "I thought I was ready for the roller coaster."

At the Boardwalk, Harry and Nancy walked up the long curving ramp that leads to the Giant Dipper—a roller coaster modeled after the one at Playland.

"The floor was rumbling from the train going overhead. Suddenly I didn't want to go on it," says Harry. "But I didn't want to back out, either."

"Do you hear that?" said Nancy, as the train pulled up next to them.

"Yup," said Harry, wishing he couldn't hear a thing.

"This is our train. Let's go!"

Harry got in next to his sister and pulled the metal safety bar over his legs.

"It seemed to take forever to get to the top of the hill,

creaking and clanking our way up. I thought okay, I want to get out now and walk. I don't like this. But before I could think much more, our car rose over the top and we went zooming down and around a sharp turn. I had white knuckles by the time I finished, but it wasn't a horror scare. It was a thrill.

"The next time I was at the Boardwalk, I was a little bit nervous about doing it again. But I've been on that one now about 20 times. Wherever I go where there are roller coasters, that's where I head first."

Harry's enthusiasm for thrill rides has been enough to make his family wonder if he's reliving a second childhood—or maybe just refusing to grow up.

"We go over to Stonestown Shopping Center at Christmastime to have an evening out—do a little shopping, and eat dinner," says Joanne.

"Harry will actually get antsy, and ask, 'Can we go on the rides now?' The Octopus, the Heydey, the Rock-o-Plane. He never has enough rides on the roller coaster in succession. He'll just go and go and go."

Actually, Harry's a bit of a snob when it comes to thrills. He much prefers traditional wooden roller coasters to high-tech steel machines. And he's disdainful of the 'twirly-whirly' rides, which he says, play stomach-churning gravitational tricks on riders.

"They can make you feel like you're doing something you're not really doing. There's one that holds you against a wall by centrifugal force, then drops the floor about ten feet below you. You're stuck to the wall going around and around with nothing underneath you. All it does is make me dizzy and sick."

Harry prefers good, old-fashioned roller coasters. The steeper and faster, the better. His favorite is the Texas Giant at Six Flags Over Texas near Dallas. Written up in *Smithsonian* magazine as the world's largest freestanding roller coaster, the 130-foot-high wooden contraption hurls its passengers over 23 crests and gullies.

"Most roller coasters have maybe 10 dips, and last about a minute. This one is just over three," he says. "It seems to go on forever, throwing you off your seat all the time. It gets going so fast, you feel them putting on the brakes twice during the ride to slow it down."

Wooden roller coasters are more exciting, says Harry, because, even though they are safe, carefully engineered machines, they sound like they're going to fall apart at any minute.

"The new modern ones made of steel go upside down and do loops, and are fun, but there's nothing like the old wooden ones," he says. "The wood rattles and vibrates. The noise makes you feel like you're going faster than you really are. The whole mood is set by the rhythmic roar of the thing going over dips."

Another of Harry's favorites is the Colossus at Magic Mountain, just north of Los Angeles. Harry describes the 120-foot coaster as "a good, long ride."

He was the eyes—or at least the narrator—of the Colossus for a group of blind kids competing in the USABA Olympics in Los Angeles. After the competition, the group went to the amusement park. Harry couldn't wait to share his expertise.

"These kids really looked up to Harry because he's done everything," said Ed La Buy, president of the Oakland chapter Optimist Club, the group sponsoring the trip. "He'd take everyone on the rides, then explain to them what's happening. It's a lot of fun to have Harry yelling just as they're going over the top, 'Okay, kids, now we're going to take a 150-foot DROP!"

There is one "twirly-whirly" ride that has made it into Harry's portfolio of favorites: the Orleans Orbit at Great America. The ride features a series of cars suspended from a wheel that rotates fast enough for centrifugal force to hold riders in their seats as they swing in 360-degree loops—without any kind of safety bar to keep them from falling out.

Harry has ridden it more times than he can count at Great America in Santa Clara, California.

"I told my blind friend, Mike McAviney, about it, and he didn't believe that it was possible to go upside down without falling out of the seat. Think about what happens when you swing a bucket of water over your head. If you do it fast enough, not a drop will spill out. It's the same thing on the Orleans Orbit."

Harry must have made the explanation convincing enough, because Mike agreed to go on the ride with Harry.

Afterward, Mike still didn't believe Harry—he didn't feel that they had gone upside down at all.

"You went head over heels three or four revolutions before we came down again," Harry explained to his friend. "Remember when we started going real fast how thick the seat cushion was, about four inches? Then remember how it squished down? That was centrifugal force taking over for gravity. Instead of dropping out of our seats when we were upside down, we were pushed into them.

"So, now that you know what it does to you," Harry asked his friend, "Do you want to go on it again?"

"No thanks," Mike replied. "My stomach's still going around on the last one."

ROLLER COASTER

A roller coaster can be fun,
Although it's not for everyone.
Some people say it's quite a ride;
While others think it's suicide.
You climb the hill with a clickety-clack,
And realize you can't turn back.
You think you must have been insane
To let them lock you in that train.

You've reached the top, what can you say?
There isn't even time to pray.
You pause a moment, then you drop,
And leave your stomach at the top.
It's down and up, and down once more.
You hang on 'til your hands are sore.
The folks up front don't seem to care.
They've got their hands up in the air.

I think it's really kind of neat
The way it throws you off the seat;
And when it flings you 'round the bend,
You know your life's about to end.
But never fear—you won't go far.
Thank God, they have a safety bar.
A minute more, or maybe two,
And then—Oh nuts! the ride is through.

You'd exit quickly if you could,
But nothing works the way it should.
Your legs are like a rubber band.
They don't support you when you stand.
The ground keeps rocking like a boat.
Your heart is still up in your throat.
And after all is said and done,
Can you believe, we call this fun?!

—Harry Cordellos

Chapter 10

CRESTING THE WAKE

*"When Harry was water-skiing to Santa Catalina Island,
I saw fins about 100 yards away, getting closer and closer.
I didn't want to tell him there was a shark following him, so
I kept on saying, 'Harry, if you want to rest, get in the boat.'
When we finally pulled him aboard, those fins were about
15 feet away. The next day they caught a 500-lb. great
white in the area. Harry wasn't the least fazed, but I
kidded him that I was going to use him as bait."*
—Bob Nordskog, Publisher, *Powerboat* Magazine

In August of 1985, Harry called up entrepreneur and
boat-racing champion Bob Nordskog and said, "Okay,
I'm ready to go again."

It had been two years since the publisher of *Powerboat
Magazine* and CEO of Nordskog Industries had heard from
Harry. The last time they were together, Bob had towed
Harry behind his 38-foot cabin cruiser, hoping that his
friend would be the first blind water-skier to ski from the
shore at Long Beach in southern California to Santa
Catalina Island. Harry was far from successful at
negotiating the 31 1/2-mile channel of choppy, wind-
swept wakes.

"He fell about halfway, then went a few miles more
and fell again. Then he started falling every few hundred
feet," said Bob. "I finally drove him in. He was really
exhausted."

Water-skiing between Catalina and Long Beach was
one challenge that seemed out of Harry's reach. Hours of
balancing on a water-ski was a daunting task for him. The
constant pull of the tow handle made his hands and
arms cramp. Without sight, he was lacking a vital tool for

detecting changes in water or weather conditions. He had to rely on people in the boat or on shore to warn him about obstacles in his path. His body had to react instantaneously to whatever he skied through, around, or over.

Harry was discouraged and frustrated by his failure to complete the run. Bob, eager to be a cheerleader for Harry and his dream, offered some pragmatic advice:

"I told him if he wanted to do it again, he'd have to train. I took him home with me, and showed him the gyrations he had to go through—to tie a ski line to a tree, lean backwards and forwards, backwards and forwards to build the strength in his arms and back.

"It worked. Two years later, I took him over to Catalina and he looked awfully good, very strong. It was obvious he had prepared himself mentally and physically. He had a much better shot at success."

This time Harry would try the channel in the opposite direction, heading into the breakers at Long Beach. The boat took off from Avalon, on the east side of Catalina Island, just after dawn. The water was smooth and glassy, the air still and damp from morning fog that promised to burn off early.

Bob, then 72, was driving the same 38-foot cabin cruiser, *Ellie's Boat Too*, named after his wife. His grandson Eric was on board as Harry's eyes, along with Elmore Nelson to time the crossing, and a reporter from the *Los Angeles Times*.

Harry put on a yellow life jacket, jumped off the back of the boat into the chilly Pacific swells, and slid his feet into his single ski as members of the crew called out, "Good luck, Harry!"

He floated behind the boat, feet buoyant from the ski, for just a moment before taking hold of the tow line and yelling, "Okay Bob, hit it!"

"The thought that went through my mind was, Just stay with it until it's over," Harry remembers. "Bob and everyone else had put so much into it, and I didn't want to fail this time. I just wanted to finish before the rough water came or fatigue set in. I had done all I could do. It was in God's hands."

Harry had done more than train for the event. He had designed and built his own water ski. Harry had made his first pair of skis at the Orientation Center for the Blind, by soaking wooden boards in garbage cans full of water for five days, and shaping them by hand. At California State University, Hayward, Harry used steam to bend wood over a form to build a single ski for slalom runs. He sealed the hard ash wood with Varathane and bolted a binding to the center.

"After I made that one, I couldn't even get up on it for a while. I just about gave up on slalom skiing," Harry says with a laugh. "Eventually I learned that I had the wrong equipment on it, so I reshaped the ski by hand, grinding it down a bit. Then I put a proper binding on it, in the proper place. It made the difference. I knew it could get me to Long Beach."

Bob and his crew watched as Harry rose out of the water and leaned back, the wake furrowing up like a wall of water alongside him. He looked relaxed and confident, his form graceful and easy.

"Harry has fantastic balance," Bob said. "I've pulled top-notch skiers over the years. They can go faster because they can judge their speed by sight. Harry doesn't have that luxury, but he certainly has capabilities that I had never seen before."

On his first channel run, Harry had hung on for dear life. That tension cost him energy. By his second try, he had learned to shift his weight around to alleviate the steady pull on his arms.

"When one leg gets a little bit tired, I lean back a little more. If I feel it in my back, I push both feet forward and take all the weight in my arms."

"As we progressed across the channel," Bob remembered, "There were times I would see a strange look on his face, and I knew that he was concentrating. Then there were times I'd see him smile, and I knew he realized he was doing very well."

Harry felt strong and relaxed, sailing smoothly over the Pacific swells, passing a school of playful dolphins. No sharks this time to add unwanted excitement. "I picture the ocean as green, blue out farther, with the white foam coming at me," Harry told the *Los Angeles Times* reporter. "There is not blackness. You never lose the mental images of color."

With three miles to go, Harry got a yell from the boat that the crew could see the Queen Mary cruise ship, massive and elegant in the harbor. It was just past 7:30 a.m. The sun, burning through the fog, was reflecting off the golden dome of the Spruce Goose. This time there had been no falls—and no sharks.

"I couldn't believe we were that close," says Harry. "Foghorns normally sound pretty depressing to me, but I don't think anything sounded prettier than when I was skiing by the Queen's gate that day. It was beautiful.

"It was more exhilarating than any marathon. In running you have the crowds waving and cheering. Out there on the water, it's quieter. Just you and the spray and the waves going by. But it's exhilarating every time."

Harry hit some turbulence at the breakwater into Long Beach, and let go of the tow-line handle long enough to give his cramped hands a rest. A few moments later, he finished in style, skimming in alongside the Queen Mary with a crowd of friends and journalists cheering from the dock. He had been on water skis for one hour, 28 minutes.

"You might think it was pretty easy, because water-skiing is something I like so much. But the Catalina experience in many ways was the most difficult thing I've ever done. We'd bitten off such a big challenge," he says.

"I didn't realize how much excitement and emotion was involved until I let go of the handles at the end. It was such a feeling of exhilaration, mixed with a pang of sadness. I had done it successfully, but I was also letting go of the thrill of a lifetime."

On the dock, Harry shook the hand of another of his heroes. World class water-skier Chuck Sterns not only congratulated Harry on his skiing, but on the craftsmanship of his water ski as well.

"To make a product that is outstanding, then have it admired by Chuck Sterns after such a performance, well, Harry could never have been happier," Bob says.

"When Harry climbed out of the boat at the end of the event, the look on his face was absolutely marvelous. It was a look of happiness and total accomplishment. He has so much to contribute to this world, to people who are unfortunate in some regard, whether it be because of a lack of sight or not. To me, he's simply an inspiration."

When Bob Nordskog died after suffering a stroke in July 1992, Harry knew he had lost more than a fan. He had lost a friend and a mentor.

"He was so enthusiastic from the beginning," Harry remembers. "We met at an Optimist Club reception in Los Angeles. What started out as a casual remark about water-skiing turned into a real project, a mutual goal.

"Bob had pulled many of the top skiers for years as part of the Catalina Challenge speed races, and he was convinced that I could do it. He had a lot of confidence in me, and made me feel that I was part of that crowd of elite athletes."

Harry will do just about anything to water-ski. He may be known for his running accomplishments, but water-skiing—the activity that pulled him out of the self-defeatist quagmire of his childhood—is his first love. It is more akin to a calling than a hobby.

"Every time I get up on skis, it's just as exciting as the first time," says Harry, with a big smile as he loads a ski onto a friend's boat. He knows he's about to spend a day saying, "Hit it!"

Grant Garl met Harry in 1983 at Camp Mather, a family camp in the Sierra foothills. The first time Grant saw Harry, he wasn't exactly recognizable. Harry was out in the middle of the lake, his head covered with a crown of wet, slimy seaweed. A group of kids swam around him, squealing whenever the "Green Monster" made a move.

Grant didn't know Harry was blind until he heard someone on shore yell a warning about drifting too far out.

"I told my girls that there was a blind man swimming in the lake, and they wouldn't let it alone. They kept asking questions, so we went over to the campfire that night and introduced ourselves," Grant says. "The kids just keyed into him right away. Then they showed the movie of him doing the Dipsea run. I just couldn't believe it."

After a week at Camp Mather, Grant offered to take Harry water-skiing at Lake Pillsbury in California.

"He said he'd check his calendar, then cancel any plans he had. He just loves water-skiing. I think Harry's greatest handicap is other people, because he has to depend on others to do things, and he can't really reciprocate."

Harry's water-skiing trip with the Garls has become an annual summer event. "He's just wonderful to have along. He does everything from washing the dishes to actually spotting from the boat."

It's hard to imagine Harry as a spotter, but he observes with his hands. By holding on to the tow rope and the tow post in the center of the boat and feeling the angle of the rope, he can tell where the skier is, as well as coach the skier about holding the rope too high or too low.

When Harry is the "eyes" of the boat, he always makes sure that someone else is the official observer, since it's the law in most states for someone to be watching the water-skier and giving signals at the first sign of danger.

"I don't know if there's a law against me being the observer, but we're not going to push it," says Harry.

On a warm, almost humid day in September, Harry caught a ride up to Discovery Bay to visit Phil Paulson, a retired fire-engine mechanic living in a housing development nestled in the channels of California's Delta.

Harry and Phil are regular water-ski buddies, enjoying the often balmy weather and flat waters of the narrow, protected delta channels.

"He'll carry his water skis 75 miles on public transportation to get up here," says Phil. "It seems odd to see a blind person carrying all that gear and using a cane, but he does what he has to do. His enthusiasm is quite unusual. He's driven when it comes to water-skiing."

Harry has visited Phil enough times to know the layout of the house. He does minor cooking and always helps wash the dishes.

"And he does a good job, too," Phil says, laughing. "He always wants to pitch in. I forget he's blind when he comes up here. He'll walk down to the dock, somehow know when he's getting near the end and dive off by himself. He'll even swim by himself and listen for sounds to tell him where he is."

Indian Summer is Harry and Phil's favorite time of year in the Delta. The usual summer crowds have thinned, it's still hot out, and the water is still warm enough to forgo wet suits.

Harry had schlepped his cumbersome load of gear on a two-hour bus ride from San Francisco to the hills east of Berkeley, and piled everything into Jane McClelland's car for the drive to Discovery Bay.

Harry couldn't wait to get there and show off his new toy, a contraption called an "air chair" that allows skiers with enough guts and balance to rise a few feet above the water and shush along on a thin stand of metal.

The 35-pound chair, developed in 1989, puts the skier in a sitting position, belted in at the waist and ankles, with the feet strapped to a wide, single ski. Under the ski is a three-foot long metal stand connected to a flat foil. As the boat pulls the ski towards the surface, the skier leans back enough to get the ski tip out of the water. Then comes the fun part, as the forward momentum pulls the foil to the surface and the skier flies along on top of the water.

"Riding the air chair is three-dimensional water-skiing. Not only do you have the yaw and pitch side-to-side and back and forth, you also go up and down," says Harry, demonstrating the movement of the chair with his hands.

"It's really like flying a plane, with take-offs and landings. The air chair wants to fly. It wants to leave the water. And once it does, there's no more sound. That's what's so neat. It's quiet. You go over whitecaps and you can't even feel it."

After a warm-up run on Phil's slalom ski, Harry bolts the air chair together and drops it over the side of the boat. He straps himself in and yells, "Hit it" to Phil. Within seconds he's above the wake, smiling and relaxed.

He explains the technique to Phil and Jane, using his hands to demonstrate how body position keeps the chair from flipping backwards or forwards.

"You fly the chair with your whole body, using your hips, feet, hands, head," Harry says. "Leaning even a few inches can make a big difference in balance."

After three tries, Phil, who has been slalom skiing with ease since the 1940s, could barely get the air-chair ski tip out of the water before falling to the side. Jane, a novice skier, surprised herself by getting the chair a few feet out of the water and skimming along before hitting the surface with a splash.

Harry gets on the air chair for the ride back to the dock. He seems to float, moving up and down on the foil like a carnival ride for almost three miles. He is smooth and effortless, with a look of pure enjoyment on his face as he turns the wake into wings of water splashing on either side of him.

"You make it look so easy," says Jane, as Harry climbs back into the boat.

"That thing is the greatest, it's just a great ride. It's the only thing I like better than roller coasters," he exults as he and Phil hoist the ski into the boat. "It took me a year to learn to fly it. By next year, I hope I'll be jumping it. You lean back to pop it in the air, then land on the foot of the foil. But it's easier said than done."

Phil and Jane look at each other and shake their heads. It might seem improbable, even a little crazy. But neither has any doubt that Harry and his chair will soon be airborne.

Harry and his water skis have created wide-eyed amazement for years. It's not just that he's eager and enthusiastic about the sport. Nor is it just that he's a gutsy blind athlete. When it comes to water-skiing, Harry simply has talent. He's consistently one of the top blind water-skiers in the world in his age group, winning tournament after tournament. He was one of the first blind skiers in the country to try jumping and barefoot skiing. And he's a regular at Cypress Gardens in Florida, the Big Top of America's professional water-skiing venues.

"He's a good skier, period, blind or not," says Mike Suyderhoud, director of his own water-skiing center in Lake Shasta, California.

Harry went to Lake Shasta in 1987 to speak to a service club in the area, and stopped by Mike's school.

"I trick-skied with him," Mike says. "He was doing turns on the surface behind the boat, as well as some complex wake tricks, where he used the wake to get in the air, then turned around and landed backwards."

Mike, a five-time World champion water-skier, had never worked with a blind person before. It was a challenge to explain technique to Harry without relying on visuals. Instead, Mike used words and moved Harry's hands, demonstrating which direction he should move, and how his body should feel turning, edging the wake, catching air.

"He's a great example to other people who are blind as far as what can be done. He far exceeds what most people who are sighted can do, as well," says Mike. "Some people talk, some people do. Harry's one of those who gets out there and does.

"He even jumps. When you leave the ramp, you're traveling in the neighborhood of 30 feet before you land. It's very, very exhilarating. It's exciting enough with your eyes open. I just can't imagine what it's like blind. If you don't hit the jump quite right, you get launched off it, thrown around, and, boom, come down. Harry has gotten pretty banged up. He's quite gutsy."

Much as Harry loves a challenge, even he thought blind water-ski jumping was pushing the margin of sanity and safety a bit too far. He was in Perth, Australia, in 1989, representing the U.S. in the World Water-ski Tournament for the Disabled, when he heard blind skiers on the British team talking about the thrill of jumping.

"We thought they were crazy," he says, with a laugh. "No one in the U.S. would consider letting a blind person hit that ramp at 25 miles per hour. But the British took their coach and their lake time to teach the rest of the world how to jump."

First Harry—and the few other skiers willing to try—learned jumping techniques on dry land with British Coach, Peter Felix.

"He had us jumping off picnic tables to get a feel for being in the air. Then he told us to assume the starting position by thinking of a threatening ape hunched over, with its hands out as if it were going to shake hands with somebody."

The skiers went out on the boat to listen as the British blind skiers jumped, and Harry held the ropes from the boat to feel the angle of the pull.

"Before I knew it, I was in the water, holding on to the tow handle," Harry says.

Peter skied alongside Harry, giving him a countdown to the ramp, a three-foot-high incline coated with fiberglass, then slicked with wax and running water.

"'You've got 200 meters to go,' he said, and I figured, Gee, I'm going to be alive for 200 more meters. Then he said, 'One hundred meters, you're looking great.' By now, all I could hear was my heart pounding. 'Get ready,' he said, 'Three... two... one... freeze,' and skied off to the side.

"Then the world stood still for 25 seconds as I waited to slam into the monster, and, in theory, go over the top, glide gracefully down and ride away in victory. I did it exactly like that the first time, and I was so shocked, I fell over backwards."

Florida's Cypress Gardens, one of the oldest and biggest professional water-ski shows in the country, has been showcasing the sport for more than 50 years. Winter Haven, with its balmy, year-round sunshine and chain of warm fresh-water lakes is known as the water-skiing capitol of the world. The Gardens draw more than 800,000 visitors a year, and always feature the world's most daring and talented skiers.

Harry first heard about the place in 1955, during a big-screen Cinerama show in San Francisco.

"It was the same day I got turned on to roller coasters. But the water-skiing sequence was too much. The force of speed and water seemed crazy. So it was also the day I decided they would never strap those boards on my feet and drag me behind a powerboat," Harry laughs.

By 1980 of course, Harry had changed his mind about water-skiing. He went to Florida in November to visit Fred Horrell, a friend who had just established the Christian Family Ski School in Winter Haven. Fred took Harry to Cypress Gardens to watch a performance, and surprised him by arranging for the Gardens to dedicate the show to Harry.

"Afterward, one of the show directors, Suzanne Curry, came up and asked if I would like to ski that afternoon," Harry says. "My response was, 'How long do I have to go home and get a bathing suit?'"

Suzanne gave Harry a new suit and introduced him to Jimmy Cassata, a U.S. Navy lieutenant and one of the head skiers at the Gardens, who was to be Harry's guide.

"It was a very cold day, and not many people wanted to get in the water," says Jimmy. "But Harry didn't care how cold it was. He just wanted to get out there and do it.

"Harry exudes confidence. He doesn't just say, I'd like to try it. He says, 'I'm going to try it and make it.' He gets a lot of doors opened that way. If he were timid or scared, people would think he'd get hurt. But he's an athlete."

Harry returned to San Francisco exhilarated. He had found ski heaven—a place where people lived, breathed, and ate water-skiing.

"Then Fred called me and said that the Gardens owners wanted me to ski in the show on Thanksgiving Day. It was too late to make it back to Florida in time, which was disappointing. But the good news was that I had a standing invitation to ski there—and not just after the shows, but *in* the shows," Harry says.

It's an invitation that Harry has accepted with enthusiasm and anticipation year after year.

"It's great for the Gardens," says show director Mark Voisard. "There are enormous public relations benefits around a person like Harry, and his abilities and insights into life. Harry doesn't take any baby-sitting. We take him where he needs to be and tap him with the tow rope and he takes off. He waves to the crowd, and everyone just eats it up. Harry will agree that the best part is getting to show off."

More than 2,000 people watch Harry when he makes his guest appearances. Even so, he says the pressure doesn't get to him—he's having too much fun. He'll start with some relaxed, graceful slalom skiing, then go for the fancy turns, tricks, and even some air-chair stunts. Often his jump attempts end with a splashy fall, but he always gets up smiling. Then he'll ski back to the amphitheater and talk to the crowd.

"People get really excited by him. They're just amazed that someone without sight can ski so well," Jimmy says.

"He's a lot better than most recreational skiers. His form is excellent, even in rough water. There were three-foot waves blowing across the lake during a few shows, and he still went out. He just can't seem to get enough skiing. He always does all four shows, then practices in between. Then he wants me to take him out running afterward. I can't keep up with him.

"He gets around so well, I got to wondering a couple of times if he could see just a little. He'd be on my arm, and there I was practically walking him off the dock or tripping him over the ropes and skis and steps that are around a pier. I'd say, 'C'mon, Harry, tell me the truth. You're not just legally blind? He'd laugh and joke around, saying, 'Hurry up, I want to see the next show.'"

Harry was the first blind person to try the Cypress Gardens jump ramp—at six-feet, higher and steeper than most.

"I didn't see how he could do it," says Jimmy, who was the first at the Gardens to guide him over the jump. "When he hits the jump, there's a tremendous impact. He can't see to brace himself, and I thought he would just buckle right into it. It's a total surprise to him, and so is the landing. He'll be flying through the air and not know when he'll hit the water.

"If he's not perfectly over his skis, he'll slip sideways and flip over. He often takes a beating, but he's landed a few good jumps. Harry paved the way for jumping to be done by blind skiers at the Gardens."

"Banana" George Blair is a legend among legends at Cypress Gardens. The 77 1/2-year old water-skier always skies barefoot, and he always wears yellow, a color he says stands out in his mind as so attractive that he's drawn to it like a magnet. Indeed, with yellow skis, yellow wet suit, yellow life jacket, Banana George looks like a bright spring flower shooshing along the top of the water.

But barefoot skiing isn't for those with soft feet, or backs or knees or arms. Banana George has broken his ribs four times, and has put more than a few dents and cracks in his back, knees, and fingers.

"You go two to three times as fast barefooting as you do with skis," he says. "The falls that we take put it in the category of contact sports equal to football and soccer. When you're on skis and you fall, you stay on top of the water and slow down gradually. Barefooting, when your foot goes through the surface, your momentum stops immediately and your body gets slammed into the water."

Harry, of course, thought it sounded fun. He tried it in 1980 at Fred's ski school. And in 1991, he was one of a group of blind skiers who decided it was time to shed their skis and take a lesson from Banana George.

"I didn't do much barefooting," says Harry. "When you fall, it's like hitting a brick wall. It really beats you up. But it's definitely exciting. There are a few blind people who do it, but I don't know if many do it well."

Harry learned to barefoot ski by holding onto a bar sticking out from the side of the boat; the solid pole supported his weight until he could get his heels in the correct position to skim the water. Then he tried holding onto a short rope that kept him ahead of the wake, which is tricky to negotiate without skis. He has yet to barefoot behind the boat with a long rope, but Harry has managed to ski backwards using the bar—a stunt that impressed his teacher.

"Can you imagine skiing without sight? I can't," says George. "I told people recently that I was going to do an exhibition at a national blind tournament, and they broke out laughing. They didn't understand that these people can see without eyes. They feel. The announcer describes what we are doing, and they feel and see in their own mind's eye exactly what I'm doing at all times.

"Barefooting is a thrill to teach someone, and Harry was one of the early birds who was willing to try it. My hat's off to him."

It seems unbelievable, but in all of Harry's athletic feats in water and on land, he had managed to avoid anything more than an array of minor bumps and bruises in the way of injuries. Until the spring of 1992, that is, when a water-skiing tow line broke his lucky streak.

In May, Harry went out to do some practice runs the day before the Masters Disabled Tournament near Jackson's Gap, Alabama.

"The fellow ahead of me hadn't landed one jump, and I thought, Aw, heck, this is going to be an easy tournament. There didn't seem to be any competition for me, but after listening to the guide count down for the other skiers, I figured I could get some good jumps in. The guide had a real even cadence calling out numbers, so I'd have an accurate idea of when I'd hit the ramp.

"I probably made one of my best jumps ever. But then I dipped my right ski tip just before landing, and it caught on the water and pitched me forward. Falls like that are a dime a dozen, but somehow my right hand got down inside the triangle of the ski rope handle, and the momentum of hitting the water threw my hand back toward my feet. Then the boat got up to the speed I was going and snapped my arm forward with a vicious jerk."

Harry bobbed up to the surface, his life jacket keeping him buoyant. At first he thought he wasn't hurt since he felt no pain.

"I thought, Gee, I almost had an accident. Then I shook my head a little to make sure I was in my right mind, and went to raise my hands up to wave to the boat operator that I was safe. I could only feel one hand. It's hard to describe the feeling I had inside, groping around, hoping to find my hand somewhere on the surface of the water. I wondered if it had gotten left back by the jump. When I found it, it was like touching another man's hand. It was still connected to my arm, but I had no sensation that something was touching it.

"When the boat circled by, I calmly said, 'I think I broke my arm.' They pulled me in and got me on the dock. By that time the swelling was just unbelievable, and feeling in it was coming back. Boy, was it painful!"

Harry went to a nearby hospital for X-rays, and found out that he hadn't broken any bones, but he had severely bruised just about every muscle in his arm. The tremendous pull of the tow handle had torn part of his biceps away from the shoulder bone.

"I totally demolished the ski handle. It was bent like a 'V.' The guys from the tournament offered it to me as a souvenir, but I didn't want any reminder of how bad it was. I want to think of jumping as good."

In fact, Harry said he wanted to go back to the lake immediately and jump in the tournament. That raised a few eyebrows, as Harry's doctors assured him that jumping—or any other kind of water-skiing—was out of the question for at least a month.

Harry was too full of painkillers to protest, and simply decided not to mention that he was heading for Boulder, Colorado, in a few days to be a celebrity runner at the Bolder Boulder 10K with New York Marathon winner Priscilla Welch. When it comes to bed rest and recuperation, patience is a virtue Harry has yet to master.

By the time he arrived in Boulder, his arm was still twice its normal size and the slightest jar against it was painful. Even Harry had to admit he was in no shape to run six miles. Besides, at his doctor's prudent suggestion, he had already mailed his running gear home from Alabama.

Harry moped around his hotel room until Priscilla walked in with her husband's running shoes—size 12, a perfect match for Harry.

"I've decided you didn't come all this distance to run this thing and then sit in your room and do nothing," she told Harry. "We'll do the six-mile striding course. If you can't finish, we'll just step off the course and take the shuttle bus back to the stadium."

Harry immediately brightened, and set a goal for finishing in two hours, giving himself a relaxed 20 minutes per mile.

"We ended up finishing in one hour, 24 minutes, and that's with no arm swing," Harry says. "Now I'm tempted to stride one of these races officially to see what I can really do."

Five days after the accident, Harry arrived back in San Francisco, where doctors at Kaiser Medical Center worried that the stubborn swelling would cut off circulation to his fingers. They told him to expect a permanent 30-percent decrease in strength in his injured biceps. Harry tried not to worry about the prognosis; instead, he walked on his treadmill, swam at the YMCA pool, and soaked in the Jacuzzi, letting the heat and bubbles soothe his battered muscles. It took weeks for the swelling to disappear.

Harry's fall would have been enough to keep many people away from water-skiing for awhile. Not Harry. He couldn't wait to get back on the jump ramp.

"I'll be nervous when I go out there again. But I want to do it, because, to me, the scariest, most dangerous part of water-ski jumping for blind people is not what happened to me. The chance of that happening again is about as likely as winning the lottery. What's worse is that people see someone like me have an accident, then decide it's too dangerous for blind people to be out there.

"I really don't believe that the Lord let me have such a wonderful gift in life, only to be hurt doing the very thing that gave me so much confidence. There's no limit to what is possible when people say, 'Yes, you can.'"

Harry was back on skis within six weeks. He took his new air chair to an annual summer water-skiing retreat at Fallen Leaf Lake in California, sharing in the excitement as he taught blind and sighted people how to fly the chair.

In August 1992, he made the U.S. Disabled Water-ski Team, and will head to France in 1993 to compete in slalom, trick, and jump skiing. In October 1992, he traveled to Florida for the American Blind Skiers Tournament at Sonesta Village Resort.

"This was the first time I really put my arm to the test, and it's a long way from recovered," he says. "Now that the swelling is gone, you can see where the bicep came loose and hangs down in the arm like a lump."

As Harry flew over the jump ramp and did his turns and tricks in the wake, his sore arm could barely grip the handle.

"I didn't land any jumps, but I came close. And I still got some of the best runs I've had. I'm not going to use my arm as an excuse. I've just got to strengthen it and make the rest of the muscles compensate. It will take some time, but I honestly think I'll be water-skiing when I'm 80 years old."

Harry's arm may have kept him from nailing the jumps in competition, but he didn't let the soreness stop him from adding yet another entry to his portfolio of athletic 'firsts.'

"In March 1993, after wowing the Cypress Gardens crowds with his slalom and air-chair antics, Harry heard director Michele Morris describe the show's grand finale: a four-tier pyramid of water-skiers.

"That has to be spectacular," Harry told her, visualizing a graceful mountain of skiers skimming around the stadium.

"You could do that," Michele said. "How about being the outside man on a three-tier formation?"

"Don't think I'd refuse," Harry told Michele.

The next thing Harry knew, it was the final show of the day, and he was heading down to the dock with the other skiers, dressed in a royal blue sequined bodysuit.

"I thought, 'How in the world am I going to do this with no practice and no strength in one arm.' If anything went wrong and I missed the start or didn't have the muscle to hang on, the whole thing would collapse."

Harry stepped in with the line of skiers and the boat pulled eleven people off the dock at once. The start was perfect, and the group looped behind the stadium to get in position before appearing in the show circle.

I could feel all the girls climbing up to form the top tier," Harry says. "I was squeezing to hold the base together. We had it all built up and under control, and went right under the grandstand before counting down and letting go. Everyone just loved it!"

"It was as much fun as anything I've done anywhere," says Harry, his voice revealing the excitement and thrill of the experience. "What those people did for me down there—to my knowledge, there has never been a disabled skier involved in a show pyramid before. You talk about no limits!"

For the folks at Cypress Gardens, Harry is the perfect role model, especially for people who see themselves as not in perfect health, says Jimmy Cassata.

"People are just flabbergasted by Harry," says Jimmy. "Fear is one of the biggest factors in life that stops people from doing things. But watching Harry go over the jump or do wake tricks gives people hope that, no matter what, you can overcome your limitations."

Chapter 11

NEVER SAY NEVER

"Just after my right eye had to be removed in 1979,
I went windsurfing for the first time. I was on my hands
and knees on the board after being blown all over the place
and swallowing half of the San Francisco Bay, and I
shook my head as hard as I could to clear my ears. I felt
something bounce off my forehead and cheek, and I
reached up to wipe the water from my face—and, no
eyeball! I had shaken out my brand new eye! I hadn't
even made a down payment on it yet. But the man upstairs
must have been watching, because I put my hand down
on the sail, and my fingers landed right on my eye.
So I always tell people, 'When you go wind surfing,
be sure to keep your eye on the sail.'"
—Harry Cordellos

Harry's feet, clad in tight-fitting boots with smooth, black rubber soles, are balanced on ledges no wider than a finger. He holds himself on the vertical wall rising 30 feet over his head, with one hand gripping a piece of textured plastic molded into the shape of a small rock. The other hand sweeps the wall in search of something—anything to hold onto.

"Next to your head, about a foot to the left is a big knob," the instructor at CityRock Climbing Gym near Berkeley, California, tells Harry.

Knees trembling from the strain of standing on the micro-edges, Harry moves his left hand up, and curls his fingers around the pebbly hold bolted into the wall. This is Harry's first attempt at rock climbing.

"I've talked to a couple of blind people who have tried climbing. It's a lot more strenuous than I imagined," says

Harry, just before he moves his foot in search of another ledge. He misses, and, arms tired from hanging on, he pops off the wall.

"I can see how it takes balance, as well as strength," he laughs, as he dangles from the end of the rope.

In rock climbing, it seems that Harry's blindness would work to his advantage for once. The biggest challenge for most first-time climbers is conquering their fear of heights. It's disconcerting, and often terrifying, for beginners to look down at that yawning expanse of air underneath them. Harry can't see the pieces of crushed rubber tires far beneath his feet, but that doesn't help him much. He knows he's higher than he wants to fall.

"My internal altimeter says I'm about 30 feet up. I can tell the roof is closer by the sound bouncing off it. Are you sure this rope will hold me?"

It's a good thing Harry is a master at trusting other people. He's had years of experience in relying on partners to guide him over water-skiing jump ramps, over curbs and around trees in marathons, through choppy ocean swells while swimming. Harry knows that the instructor is holding a rope that is tied to the harness around his waist. Even so, there is a moment of hesitation at the top when the instructor tells him to let go of the wall and lean back, letting the rope take his weight.

"You can really hold me? All 176 pounds?"

"No problem," says the instructor, a slender young woman. She lets the rope out through a metal device, and Harry glides slowly back to solid ground.

Harry walks a few steps forward and puts his hands back on the holds.

"That's not the same one I started with last time. Where's that nice big one?" he asks, moving his hand to the left. "There, that's better."

Harry remembers the sequence he did before and passes the point where he fell off. The instructor calls out directions. Harry's balance, strength, and sense of direction get him to the top, where he rings a cowbell, making an echoing clang throughout the gym.

"Hey!" Harry calls down from the top of the wall.

"That was much easier the second time. I could do it blindfolded."

Getting Harry to try a new sport is easy enough, once you find a window of time when he's not running a marathon in Texas, teaching water-skiing at a Sierra mountain lake, or giving a motivational lecture to school kids in Virginia. He makes Nike's "Just Do It" advertising campaign seem like it was tailor-made for him. Harry lives for experiences.

The trouble starts when he tries to find time to pursue all of his diverse interests and talents. In addition to a hefty regimen of running and water-skiing, Harry's *curriculum vitae* is bursting at the seams with a list of athletic endeavors that includes hang gliding, windsurfing, golfing, bowling, swimming, diving, bicycling, downhill and cross-country skiing, fishing, kayaking, and ice skating. He's even a certified lifesaving and water-safety instructor.

Harry's commitment to try new things is the driving force behind his go-for-it attitude. But it doesn't mean that he plows in without hesitation. Harry does consider the risks. After all, the number of times he has fallen down, scraped his knees, and bumped his head would make anyone stop and think before diving in.

Harry's first athletic challenge was to overcome his fear of water. For his brothers and sisters, the ocean was a playground, just a block away from the house. But Harry never thought of it as a place to splash away the warm summer days. To Harry, with his fuzzy vision, water was a disorienting, bottomless expanse waiting to swallow him up. The ocean was cold and the waves knocked him off his feet, making him shiver with fear.

Twice during one summer, Harry jumped into swimming pools during family outings, only to become disoriented and thrash about in a desperate search for the sides.

"The second time, the lifeguard was angrier than if I had been throwing rocks into the pool. He pulled me out and said, 'Blind people have no business being in a pool alone,'" Harry remembers. "I knew he was wrong—being blind had nothing to do with it. I just didn't know how to swim. But his comment hit me like a brick wall."

That day, Harry vowed never to go in the water again.

"Of course," Harry says with a smile, "'Never' is one of those words we use without really meaning it."

In 1964, Harry signed up for a recreation leadership class at California State University, Hayward. His instructor, Bill Niepoth, had all the students introduce themselves by talking about their favorite recreational activity and what activity they would like to try.

"My favorite activity is water-skiing," Harry told the class. "And if I could do anything else, I'd like to learn to swim."

That elicited a few laughs of astonishment.

"You water-ski and you can't swim?" asked one student.

"I never had the chance to learn. I just wear a life preserver."

Harry became a class project. One of the students was a coordinator for the Red Cross water safety program at the Berkeley YMCA, and offered to help Harry organize a swimming class for blind people.

Harry jumped at the chance and found five other blind people to fill the class. They started in the warm, shallow, beginner's pool, getting used to the sensation of being surrounded by water.

"Without the fear of drowning and the constant shivering, learning to swim was a pleasant experience. Once I stopped panicking and thrashing around, I learned to use the water's buoyancy to hold me up."

It took a bit more time for Harry to get over his fears in the deep pool. Eight feet of water might as well have been 30 or 100, as he jumped in and scrambled for the surface and the side. The thought of being under all that water was enough to give him goose bumps, even in a heated pool.

With a little push from the instructors, Harry began to learn about orienting himself in the water. The students used lane markers to keep from veering to the side. The instructors advised the students to use the breast stroke—

which keeps the hands in front of the face and head, and allows for easy, relaxed breathing—to remove any doubt about where the edge was.

Harry realized that he had lost his fear of deep water when he bumped heads with another swimmer. Instead of panicking or thrashing, he simply reestablished his direction and continued his lap.

"After that I started to enjoy deep water. In fact, I probably spend just about as much time down on the bottom diving for metal washers as I do swimming at the surface."

Swimming became stress therapy for Harry, giving him an escape from heavy course demands and frustrating research. Sometimes an hour workout stretched to two or three as he swam away his tensions lap after lap.

One day Harry noticed that the underwater speakers had been turned on at the pool.

"I plunged into the pool as usual, and when the bubbling sound cleared, I was surrounded by music. I glided slowly down to the deepest point and then stood on the bottom looking around, visualizing the other swimmers moving in perfect rhythm with the music. In an almost weightless environment, I could swim in any direction I wanted, and in between the trips to the surface for air, I must have covered every square inch of the pool."

Swimming became a part of the fabric of Harry's life. He spent just about every free hour in the pool while he was a student, and still swims at least four or five times a week at the YMCA near his house. Within a year of his first swimming class, he passed all of the swimming tests at the Red Cross. He took courses in senior lifesaving, water-safety instruction, and scuba diving and, in 1968, received his Red Cross Lifesaving certificate. In 1976, he wrote a book on aquatic recreation for the blind, published by the National Education Association. Harry definitely had conquered his fear of water.

"When Peter bought a fishing boat in the early 1960s, Harry taught us to water-ski. That was before he learned to swim," brother Dennis remembers.

"It's funny to think back and picture him. He had such fear. He used to take 25 minutes to get in the water with a life jacket on. Now if you see him in the water, he's like a porpoise or a seal. You get him near water, and boom, he's in."

In 1970, Harry called Walt Stack to chat about the Dolphin–South End Running Club. Walt, who was president of the group at the time, is also known as San Francisco's human penguin. Until surgery slowed him down at the age of 84, Walt swam in the bay every day of the year for at least an hour.

Walt told Harry about the club's most recent event, the Golden Gate Swim. Participants start at the San Francisco waterfront, and swim under the Golden Gate Bridge to Lime Rock across the Bay in Marin. Harry was entranced by the idea of an open-water swim.

"It's pretty rough out there," Walt cautioned. "It's almost always choppy and there are big rolling swells coming in under the bridge. It's only about a mile across, but you end up swimming a lot farther by the time you fight back and forth across the currents. What gets most people though, is the cold. It's never much warmer than 58 degrees out there."

But Walt is never one to discourage athletic ambitions, especially if the plan involves swimming in the bay. He offered to guide Harry on one of the club's regular morning swims.

It was January 16 when the two met early in the morning at the Dolphin Club house. Walt and Harry stripped down to their swim trunks and headed out the door that led to the dock.

"As the door swung open, a rush of cold air hit me like a block of ice. I could hear the breakers rolling in on the beach below us. Walt told me that the water temperature was 50 degrees."

Walt described Aquatic Park, with its long curving dock and views of the Golden Gate Bridge and Ghirardelli Square. Harry couldn't think much beyond the chills running up and down his body.

"I thought about the heart murmur I had had when I was a child, and tried to convince myself that I had truly outgrown it," Harry remembers. "I had heard too many stories about people jumping into cold water and getting heart attacks from the shock."

The two walked to the beginning of the dock, where Walt took Harry's arm and guided him towards the breakers.

"Now don't just get wet and come out again. Stay in a few minutes to get over the shock, then you'll enjoy it," Walt said.

Harry felt his heart beating as he shivered in the damp, foggy air. He gasped as the first rush of icy water washed over his feet, then clenched his teeth as he let Walt guide him further into the waves.

Suddenly Harry felt himself tumbling backwards as a wave knocked him off his feet. He stood up and started into the surf as fast as his numb toes could carry him.

"Hang on a minute!" Walt said. "Are you all right?"

"Yup. But if I don't get in now, I never will. That wind is murder once you're wet!"

The two plunged into the next wave and stroked along side-by-side, with Walt giving directions in between breaths. After 35 minutes in the water, Harry and Walt warmed up in the club's sauna.

"That wasn't so bad once we got in," Harry said. "It sure beats inching my way down a boat ladder, one toenail at a time."

Walt knew he had found a fellow penguin, and nominated Harry for membership in the Dolphin Club. In the spring of 1970, he was admitted as the first blind member in the club's 93-year history.

"The members were all so enthusiastic and friendly," Harry remembers. "They had none of the traditional hang-ups about my being blind and what I could or couldn't do."

Harry became a regular at the Aquatic Park early morning swims, and competed in several open water events sponsored by the club. But his goal wasn't just to get used to cold water. Harry was aiming to swim in the shadow of the Golden Gate.

By late that summer, everyone at the club was talking about the season's finale, the Golden Gate swim. The event committee chose a date in late fall to avoid San Francisco's summer fog season. Then the committee consulted tide tables. The water in the bay is never still, but there are times when it would be humanly impossible to swim from San Francisco to Marin.

During a strong outgoing tide, anyone trying to swim across the strait would be swept under the bridge by the powerful current. The organizers tried to time the swim for the end of a strong in-going tide or the beginning of an ebb tide.

Two nights before the swim, all the entrants gathered at the clubhouse to discuss tides and strategy for slow, medium, and fast swimmers. Routes of travel were drawn on a blackboard. Harry's partner, Pete Biannucci, explained the diagram in great detail.

September 20 dawned cold, with broken clouds and light fog. Harry boarded a tugboat with Pete and the other 50 swimmers for the ride to the San Francisco side of the bridge. The swimmers took off their shirts and climbed over the tug railing onto a narrow ledge. Below Harry was six feet of air, and the chilly waters of the bay.

"Oh my God! You should see the *Harbor King*," Dolphin member Jack Bettencourt told Harry, pointing to the double-decker boat the club had hired for all the spectators.

"Everyone's on one side leaning over the rail. They're going to tip that thing over. Those people are crazy!"

Harry pictured the huge boat listing to one side, but didn't have much time to worry. He heard the swimming commissioner's voice over the tug's loudspeaker:

"Swimmers, take your mark. Get set. Go!"

Harry stepped off, and went deep into the cold water, losing his swimming cap for a moment. The water was calm and Pete and Harry swam at an easy pace. Pete told Harry they were passing the south tower, and explained the necessity of staying well clear of the choppy, swirling water at the base that sucks inward like a whirlpool.

When Pete announced that they were mid-span, Harry began to think ahead to the jelly doughnuts and hot coffee waiting for him on the other side.

"We're exactly 2,000 feet from Lime Rock. Not bad for 30 minutes," Pete said.

"I thought we'd be finished in 35 minutes," said Harry, his confidence ebbing. "What's taking so long?"

"The tide's getting stronger. Just keep swimming. You're doing fine."

Harry pulled and kicked. The swells became rougher and the water began breaking over his head. Harry was beginning to get cold.

"I felt like a ping-pong ball being tossed about in a wild river," he remembers. "I think being blind actually offered an advantage. If I had seen any of the landmarks around us, I would have known that the current was carrying us right off course."

Harry knocked into pieces of driftwood and seaweed, and Pete told him that they were only 150 yards from Lime Rock.

"It doesn't seem like far, but the current is really beginning to move. You'll have to swim harder."

Harry pulled for all he was worth, gaining only 25 yards in five minutes.

"That can't be possible!" he sputtered to Pete.

"You've already made it across the Golden Gate, but the tide is sweeping us towards Oakland and Berkeley. We're getting farther and farther from Lime Rock."

"I'll settle for an unofficial finish," Harry said, exhausted by the water's pull. "Let's head for the boat."

After 90 minutes in the water, Harry didn't want any jelly doughnuts. He wanted to stop shivering. He huddled by the tug's engine-room boilers to stave off the shivering, sipped coffee laced with brandy, and decided to turn his disappointment into verse.

LIME ROCK BLUES

There is a place they call Lime Rock,
Upon a distant shore.
And hard against its jagged face,
The mighty breakers roar.
And every year, we Dolphin Swimmers
Choose an Autumn date,
And just to touch that slimy rock,
We swim the Golden Gate.
I still recall that first attempt,
My confidence was high.
The chilly water flattened,
as the sun broke through on high.

A touring boat, the Harbor King,
Was filled with guests that day.
They heard the starter holler, "Go!"
And we were on our way.
The dive was good, the water cold,
But smoother than a mirror.
I knew with every stroke I took,
Lime Rock was getting nearer.
I thought of celebrating,
Riding homeward on the tug,
And thought of jelly doughnuts,
and hot coffee in a mug.

But underneath the mighty span,
Flat water ceased to be.
It boiled and churned about so much,
You couldn't water-ski.
There wasn't any stopping now,
No place to take a seat.
The only place to take a rest
Was down 300 feet.
Alas! That slimy rock was near,
But yet, so far away.
I thought, if I don't touch it soon,
I'll swallow half the bay.

And after swimming 'cross the Gate,
How sad it was to me,
The current seemed to catch Lime Rock
And float it out to sea.
I stood there shocked, and treaded
In a tide I couldn't battle.
For all I knew, that crazy rock
Was headed for Seattle.
But what about the timers
And officials standing there?
To leave so soon on such a trip—
What would they eat or wear?

I headed for the waiting tug,
Too cold to even talk.
And as they helped me on the deck,
I found it hard to walk.
A couple dozen shivering men
Were standing by my side.
They really laughed and whooped it up
Throughout the homeward ride.
But silently I wondered
As we headed back to shore,
How could they be so cheerful
When Lime Rock we'd see no more.

But back on land, I learned the truth,
And man! It was a shock.
For there were the officials
And the timers on the dock.
To hear the other swimmers talk,
You'd think it was a cinch.
There's nothing wrong with old Lime Rock,
It never moved an inch!
It's really quite an honor
Just to swim the Golden Gate,
And next year, when I touch Lime Rock,
We'll really celebrate!

—Harry Cordellos

Harry was back on the boat the next year. For two weeks before the swim, Pete had picked him up at 5 a.m. for training in cold water.

"I wondered why Pete wasn't giving me any coaching on my technique," Harry remembers. "Then he told me that he couldn't see my stroke since it was totally dark during our practices. He just focused on my white swim cap to make sure I was above water."

On September 26, Harry and Pete dove into the water and settled into the rhythmic stroke they had practiced. Pete swam to Harry's left, yelling directions to keep him on course. The two were well past mid-span when the tide began to change, pushing them once again away from the finish at Lime Rock.

Harry switched to breast stroke, pulling hard. Every time his head came up for air, he got a mouthful of water. But Harry knew he was close; he could feel the swells breaking off the rock. And this time he was determined to reach his goal. He switched back to the crawl to pull harder, not even caring if he bumped his head.

"Whoa! Take it easy, you're there," he heard somebody say.

Harry's hand bumped against something hard and jagged and he stood up on a plateau at the base of the rock, spitting water out of his mouth.

"I wanted to have something to prove that I had made it, so I tried to break off a piece of the rock," he says. "I got four bloody fingers and a clump of moss in return. But that was enough."

Pete and Harry swam to the boat, where Harry shivered his way through the traditional post-swim cup of brandied coffee. This time he had a reason to celebrate, with an official finishing time of 84 minutes and six seconds. The winner that year took less than 30 minutes. But Harry will remain in the record books as the first—and, so far, only—totally blind person to finish the Golden Gate swim.

Harry hadn't let go of the bit of moss he had scraped off Lime Rock. He set the greenish clump on a shelf to dry for a few days, then with the help of a professor in the art department at Cal State Hayward, he cast it in resin. Mounted on a block of walnut, it is still Harry's most treasured trophy.

When Harry started swimming at the Cal State pool, there was one thing that bothered him: the diving board. In between the two low boards, which he used regularly to jump into the water, there loomed a three-meter board. Even standing on his tip-toes underneath it, Harry couldn't reach the springboard platform.

"I knew I would never be completely satisfied until I went off it at least once," Harry says. "I just couldn't convince myself I was ready for it."

One afternoon, Harry climbed up the metal ladder and walked out on the board between the handrails. When the rails stopped, so did Harry.

"It might only be ten feet up, but it must be at least 100 feet down," he told Dean Sutcliffe, the lifeguard who was behind him on the ladder.

Harry backed down the ladder and spent the next week obsessing about that diving board.

"It got to the point where it began to take some of the fun out of swimming," he says.

Finally, with a little push from Dean, Harry made a commitment to go off the high board. After morning classes, he met Dean at the pool, took a few warm-up laps, and climbed out of the water.

"Make your mind up that you're going off that board before you even climb the ladder," Dean advised. "If you wait until you're standing at the edge to decide, it'll be that much harder."

Harry took a deep breath and climbed up the rungs. He followed the rails, then inched his way out the last few feet to the edge. Dean told him it was clear, and Harry stepped into the air.

"It seemed like ten seconds before I hit the water," he remembers. "I was afraid of hitting the bottom, but my head popped above the surface almost immediately. The worst part had been thinking about it for a whole week."

Within a few weeks, Harry was diving from the high

board, springing as high and as hard as he could. Then he decided it was time to try somersaults.

Dean suggested that Harry wear sweats to protect his body from poor landings at that height. Harry took his advice, walked to the edge of the board, and turned around. He dropped his hands to his side and bent his knees a bit, then reached for the sky and leaned back.

"The board fell away beneath me. I felt like I was hanging in the air for a moment, then I arched over and waited to hit the bottom with a thud. But it never happened," Harry remembers. "I just splashed into the water and came back to the surface."

Harry tried the dive a few more times, then took off the sweat pants. Back flips were just the beginning. Harry quickly learned how to swan dive, jackknife, gainer (do an inward back somersault), handstand on the edge of the board, and do a whole assortment of somersaults with twists and turns. From that day on, a day at the pool would have been incomplete without a few stunts off the high board.

Watching Harry dive has an element of nerve-jangling suspense about it. The thought of a blind person willingly bouncing himself into the air and flipping around with his head precariously close to the edge of the board is enough to make most people squirm in their seats. Then there's the aspect of the crash landings when Harry doesn't quite make the move. Water makes a painful sound when a body smacks into it.

Diving spectators get their first hint that something unusual is happening the moment Harry steps up to the board. He certainly can't do the traditional running start. Instead, he gets down on his hands and knees and crawls out to the end of the board, a method he says is a fast and safe, if unorthodox, spectacle.

"Some blind people are afraid this looks silly," Harry says. "But there's nothing that looks more ridiculous than trying to pretend you're *not* blind and walking off the side of the board and scraping your elbows and shins or bumping your head on the side of the pool."

When Harry does a gainer he jumps up only once. If

he springs up and down to gain height and power, he could lose contact with the board, scrape the skin from his shins and crash into the water.

"I stand at the end of the board, facing the water, and reach for the skies at a 15- to 20-degree angle," Harry explains. "I throw my hands up as if I'm grabbing for a big rope. Then I just throw my head back and my feet go over naturally when I tuck. The tighter the tuck, the faster I go. For a double, I wait until I feel like I'm standing still in space, then I do it again.

"If I miss the timing, it's a belly or a back flop. It's like crashing through a plate-glass window. Sometimes it knocks the breath out of you."

In 1988, Harry added the 10-meter platform to his diving portfolio, when he jumped off the Olympic training tower at Indiana-Purdue University in Indianapolis.

The diving well was turned into a Jacuzzi with a bubble machine to give more cushion if Harry's jump turned into a flop. An elevator took him to the concrete platform 35 feet above the water, and he followed the railings to the edge.

"At five meters, you have time to say every prayer in the Bible before you hit the water. When you go off the 10-meter platform, you can do the Old and the New Testaments, with time to spare," he says.

"When I stepped off, it was like plunging into eternity. But when you get that nice splash, then float up, it's amazing."

Snow skiing was another sport Harry shied away from out of fear. He dreaded winter with its onslaught of cold, rainy weather that broke into his running and swimming time. But the thought of strapping a pair of skinny boards onto his feet, and whizzing out of control down ice- and snow-covered mountains made a treadmill seem like an attractive option for winter workouts.

In 1970, Harry was running in Golden Gate Park with his marathon partner, Peter Mattei. Peter invited Harry to his cabin in the mountains to try a weekend of cross-country skiing.

"I immediately made an excuse," Harry remembers. "Cross-country skiing may not be as fast as downhill, but it still seemed like just another way to break a leg."

But Harry wasn't off the hook for long. A few years later, he met Kirk Bauer at a Cal State activities festival. Kirk was displaying pictures of amputees skiing with special ski-tip runners on their poles. An amputee himself, Kirk offered to teach Harry to ski.

After talking to Kirk, Harry's fear of missing out on a new experience began to outweigh his hesitation to ski. On a January evening, Harry and Kirk arrived at the Donner Ski Ranch dormitory in Lake Tahoe for a weekend of skiing with the National Inconvenienced Sportsman's Association, a group of amateur athletes with various handicaps.

Harry had never been in snow before, and tried to imagine what it looked like outside when Kirk told him that the snowdrifts were piled high on either side of the road. Harry felt the car sliding over the mushy, slippery surface in the parking lot. He stepped out and sank four inches down, walking gingerly as he carried his gear to the lodge. He felt the cold, wet flakes in his hair and on his face.

"It didn't seem real," he says. "I thought it was something that people only dreamed up for pictures on Christmas cards."

In the morning, with cumbersome ski boots and heavy jackets, Kirk and Harry stepped outside to put on their skis.

"I could hear people zipping by as if they were going ninety miles per hour. When Kirk told me they were coming down the beginner's bunny hill, I just about went back inside."

Kirk guided Harry to a quiet, flat area, where he taught Harry to walk on skis and to step sideways. Harry learned how. to use his poles to slow himself down and steady himself, and how to point his ski tips inward in the snowplow position.

"This will keep you from going too fast," Kirk told him. "Just don't cross them, or you'll tumble head over heels. Now, lift your poles out of the snow and let yourself go forward. There's nothing to bump into."

Harry, feeling as though his skis were about to take off with or without him, snowplowed down a slight incline into the bracing oblivion. Kirk was right beside him.

"The only practical way to stop seemed to be by falling," Harry remembers. "But by late morning, we were coming down the hill and making turns, sometimes without falling at all."

Now Harry skis with relaxed abandon, skimming down hills at 30 miles per hour. His guides ski within 30 feet of him, calling out directions and warnings.

"The guide will say, 'Right,' then tell me when to turn. Or 'Left... turn. You're going onto a catwalk. Bumps ahead.' If he says, 'Stop!' I try to stop. If I don't, he'll keep saying it as long as it's safe, then yell, 'CRASH!' Then I just go right down. I can always get up again and start over with snow on my pants and sweater. You just have to be alert and learn to work with the hill, not against it.

"I've been kissed by a few branches. But only when the guide was daydreaming," Harry says, laughing. "They're only human."

By now, Harry has learned never to say never. When windsurfing instructor John Tansley offered to teach Harry his sport in 1979, his response was an enthusiastic, "Why not?" He had never set foot on a sail board before, but at least he was familiar with the chilly and choppy waters of the San Francisco Bay.

E   S   S   A   Y

"THE BLIND MAN WHO TOOK UP WIND SURFING"
by Maitland Zane
San Francisco Chronicle, 1979

Harry Cordellos, San Francisco's blind super jock, has a new sport—wind surfing.

The winds were gusty and the currents unpredictable at his sixth lesson Tuesday from John Tansley, who runs a wind surfing school at Pier 39.

As a result, the 41-year-old Cordellos spent almost as much time in the chilly bay as he did on his $750 board, sailing, with Tansley shouting instructions.

Each time he took a dunking, Cordellos scrambled back on his windsurfer, yanked the sail up out of the water and gamely tried again.

"Head up!" bawled Tansley. "Lean your mast back... now tack! Hang in there, Harry! That's it... beautiful."

Ooops.

Cordellos lost control of his mini-sailboat and flopped backwards into the water.

"I almost had it that time," he grinned, crawling back on his board for another go.

Driving the pilot boat Tuesday was Cordellos' great friend and running companion, Mike Restani, who will be at his side for Sunday's San Francisco marathon.

The two men needle each other affectionately all the time.

"Hey, Harry," Restani yelled, "The photographer wants you in front of John. The blind leading the sighted!"

The two wind surfers built up speed as they skimmed toward the land, Tansley perhaps 30 feet to the rear.

"Sheet out!" cried Tansley, who said his longest run in six years of wind surfing is a 20-mile trip from Marina Green to Coyote Point in San Mateo County.

"Sheet out... now lean the mast back! That's good... good... keep on that course..."

Uh-oh. There goes Harry again into the drink, for maybe the two dozenth time in the last 40 minutes.

"The hardest thing is keeping your balance," he said. "Wind surfing is like riding a Muni bus standing up at the rush hour, using no hands. The wind plays tricks. You expect one thing and it does another."

So far as the two know, Cordellos is the first blind person in the country to take up the sport.

"Communication is what's most important," he said, skinning out of his black rubber wet suit for a five-mile jog. "It communication fails, you're in the water. It's as simple as that."

Of all the times Harry has walked on the wild side of the sports world, his stint at hang gliding raised the most eyebrows. Buckling himself onto a couple of aluminum bars attached to a 30-foot wingspan of nylon, and soaring like a bird may have sounded reckless to some people. His mother was understandably nervous about the whole idea.

Harry got his opportunity to fly in 1975 through one of his Pamakid colleagues, Jim Vignola, who offered to team up with a professional instructor and get Harry off the ground on a tandem glider. The first day, Jim and the instructor buckled Harry into the glider and ran up and down the beach near San Francisco's Fort Funston to give him the feeling of wind and flight.

The second time, the winds were so vicious that no one was flying. So Harry got into the rig alone while four people held onto the bars and wing. The gusting winds lifted the wings enough for Harry to get a taste of gliding.

Before the three could get together again, the instructor was killed in a hang-gliding accident when his safety strap broke at 700 feet.

"That didn't scare me or make me think it was unsafe, but it did kind of sour me on the idea for a while," Harry says.

"But I've been thinking about going up in a glider at Cypress Gardens. I think a practical way to do it would be behind a powerboat, where someone can control my speed and direction, and the landings would be a lot more forgiving."

With all the activities on Harry's plate, he may worry about injury. He may worry about trying to do too much. He even may worry about how to finance his ventures. One thing Harry doesn't have to worry about is getting bored.

"I could easily fill up 24 hours a day. Sometimes it's hard to choose between so many activities. If I could be in two places at once that would solve a few problems," he says.

"But I'm not complaining. I'm lucky to have such

choices. Every time I go out and learn a new skill or rise to a challenge in a sport I already know, it's a boost for my self-confidence. I can't imagine what I'll try next. But I know better than to think I've reached my limit yet."

Chapter 12

NEW HORIZONS

"While there seem to be thousands of handicapped runners these days, Harry was one of the very first I was aware of many, many years ago. They're all inspirations, but Harry was a pioneer. True pioneers show other people that they have potential they never imagined, until they saw someone like Harry lead the way."
—Amby Burfoot, Executive Editor,
Runner's World Magazine

"Somebody has to tell people that being handicapped is not the end of the world. It can be the beginning."
—Harry Cordellos

At the Masonic Lodge in the lush, suburban hills of Orinda, California, Harry is directing the set-up of a movie screen and video and slide projectors. The lodge members are enjoying their annual Fourth-of-July evening barbeque, and the smell of hot dogs and hamburgers grilling outside wafts into the room.

Harry is in his element. He's about to sit down to his favorite all-American meal, then have the opportunity to make a difference with his message: Don't be afraid to try.

It's a simple statement, but Harry's delivery, punctuated with anecdotes and film clips of his hard-to-believe exploits, never fails to hit home.

The lights go down, and the lodge members, along with their spouses and kids, turn their chairs toward the front, where Harry is finding his way to the podium.

A picture of Harry water-skiing in the San Francisco Bay flickers on the screen. The film, shown in Europe as a segment of the "Games People Play" television show, is an impressive montage of Harry's myriad accomplishments. In it he plays ping-pong, shows how he built his carnival scene, windsurfs, rides a tandem bicycle and water-skis.

Then the film shows Harry running the Dipsea Race. There are audible gasps from the audience as people watch Harry slip-sliding down an impossibly steep, heavily wooded section of the trail behind partner Mike Restani.

"Duck, duck, duck! Rocks... over... steep... down, down, roots!" Mike yells.

Harry is wearing thick knee and elbow pads, making viewers wonder not if, but when, he'll stumble on the treacherous course.

For a few moments, there is no soundtrack, other than Harry and Mike's labored breathing, as they pound along the hills of the Marin Headlands, high above the Pacific Ocean.

"Oh, my," a woman in the audience says.

"Literally, the sky is the limit," Harry's voice narrates over shots of the two of them finishing the race—without a fall. "I can't bring back my eyesight. What I have to do is use what I have to the fullest. Don't be afraid to try. Go for it, no matter what it might be."

Watching Harry run the Dipsea Race is "an emotional trip for people," says Jim Battersby.

"People literally are exhausted watching him. They're breathing hard, and sigh with relief when he's done. Whether you're handicapped or not, you identify with Harry. You're with him on that run, and feel a sense of accomplishment when he finishes. You come out refreshed and inspired."

"I've seen Harry speak 20 times, and I've never seen an audience that didn't respond with tears and a standing ovation," Jim says. "Harry teaches people not to quit. It's part amazement and part inspiration. Everybody has excuses and fears. But you take one look at Harry and all he's accomplished and you want to go out there and do it."

In 1979, Maria Johnston was asked to take Harry on a training run around White Rock Lake before the White Rock Marathon in Dallas. A member of the Cooper Fitness

Center running club, Maria guided him around the 11-mile lake, giving him a verbal tour of the rolling hills, wooded thickets, and impressive mansions that surround the lake. Harry stayed with Maria and her husband during his visit, and has done so every year since.

"He's just super. When we're running, he makes up songs, and people are just in awe. Not only is he a blind man who passes other people, there he is singing along the way. His attitude is just fantastic. Everyone who meets him is so motivated."

Maria heard Harry speak at the Dallas Lighthouse for the Blind, to a group of parents with blind children.

"He told them how to get their children motivated and interested in sports," she remembers. "The parents were just thunderstruck. They had never imagined their children exercising. They didn't think it was possible until they heard him talk about all the things he's done."

The lights go on in the Masonic Lodge, and Harry begins to talk about ping-pong. A trivial summertime game to many, Harry explains how he turns ping-pong into a lesson about teamwork, attitude, and opportunity.

"Nobody likes to be put down as a loser, and in rally ping-pong, if you work together, you both win. The object is to keep the ball going for as long as possible, to play with somebody rather than against them.

"Next week I'll be at Camp Mather, San Francisco's family camp in the Sierras," Harry says. "People get bitten by the rally ping-pong bug, and we end up playing so late that we're hitting more mosquitos than ping-pong balls.

"When people tell me that they can't see the ball any better than I can, I know that we're playing in the dark," Harry says, eliciting laughter from his audience.

When Harry went to Washington a few years ago to run the Marine Corps Marathon, his friend Tony DeGregorio asked him to speak to his elementary school class in Reston, Virginia.

"He played rally ping-pong with the kids and they

were just amazed to see a blind man whirling around and doing tricks with the paddle," says Tony, who teaches physical education. "I've never held an assembly where they were so much in awe of what was going on. Suddenly they had an awareness of what a blind person can do. I had parents come and ask, 'Who was that guy?' because their kids would go home and talk non-stop about him."

Harry's one-time visit snowballed into an annual event. In October he spoke to hundreds of kindergarten-through-eighth-graders during 21 assemblies at eight elementary schools in Virginia.

"First I showed a video of riding the air chair. I think those kids were with me every dip," Harry says.

Then he got out the ping-pong paddles. He set up makeshift nets on library tables, kindergarten desks and cafeteria tables, and invited teachers and students to rally with him. Each player got a point for returning the ball, and five points for doing a trick before returning the ball.

Harry demonstrated his bag of ping-pong tricks: "Around the World"—passing the paddle around his body; "Under the Bridge"—passing it under his leg; "Whirly"—spinning around; and, "Drop 'N Whirly"—dropping the paddle on the table, spinning around, and picking it up.

"We had balls going in every direction," Harry says. "With every play there was a groan, because I would come so close, then miss. Then I'd get the ball the next time. It's perfect when that happens, so the kids can see that mistakes are a stop on the road to success. I tell them that the important thing is not worrying about looking silly, but to get in there and try again. We made the impossible turn into the possible.

"These kids were in their Halloween costumes ready to be in the school parade, and they sat on the gym floor for 45 minutes watching a video screen, and not moving a muscle. It's such a reward to talk to these students and see the impact that it has on them. I got letters thanking me for teaching them not to smoke. They drew pictures of ping-pong and water-skiing.

"There's no price you can put on the feeling you get when a little kid comes up and wants to shake your hand

and get your autograph. Those children never leave the auditorium with prejudices about what blind people can do. And they know they can achieve more, as well."

At the Masonic Lodge, Harry switches over to the slide projector, and pictures click onto the screen as Harry, having memorized the order, tells about each one.

Little gasps break out around the room, as the audience witnesses him doing a gainer with a twist off the high dive. He shows a picture of himself skimming along the San Francisco Bay on a rainbow-sailed windsurfer, and gets the audience laughing with his glass-eye mishap. The running picture seems a little dull—the usual snapshot of Harry in the midst of a throng of runners—until he tells the story behind it.

"The man in the green sweatsuit just on the opposite side of me is a heart-attack patient," Harry explains. "He was able to finish Bay-to-Breakers with me despite his doctor's warning that he'd never run again.

"The other man in the picture is Peter Strudwick, who was my guide in the race. If you look closely, you'll see that he has no feet. There are ways of getting around problems," he says, grinning at the understatement.

When Harry walked into a meeting of the Optimist Club of Oakland, Ed La Buy knew he'd found a built-in role model. The club does various community projects, and works with groups of youth who are at risk of falling into crime or drug use.

"A lot of these kids don't want to try something unless they know they'll succeed. They don't want to look 'uncool' in front of their friends," says Ed. "But Harry inspires them. He shows them that by not trying they're missing out on an opportunity that might be really fun.

"He doesn't let his blindness be something to be sad about, and kids respect that. He just says, 'Hey, that's the way it is. I'm not going to whimper about it. Let's go ride the roller coaster.'"

Ed himself had never imagined what it would be like to be blind until he met Harry. He signed up to play a game of beep baseball against a blind team one afternoon in a San Leandro park. "Except for the catcher and pitcher we were all either blindfolded or blind," he says.

Harry has used the game to teach classes in adapted physical education. The rules are different than standard baseball, and the balls and bases make noises to allow blind players to make unassisted field plays and swing at the ball instead of having it rolled to them on the ground.

"The ball beeps and the bases buzz," Ed says. "You have to judge the height of the ball as it's coming in by the sound. And just run towards the buzzing bases. I had to rely on my hearing and on my sense of feel. After a while I could tell if the ball was rolling towards me or bouncing. But I just wanted to duck if I was in the outfield and heard that thing coming at me with a loud, fast BEEP! BEEP!"

The blind players, says Ed, easily beat his team. "That game gave me a whole new perspective. I don't take my eyesight for granted anymore, and it showed me how much disability is an attitude. Those guys were good athletes, blind or not."

The Masonic lodge members watch "Carnival Memories," a short film Harry produced about building his festive and intricate model carnival.

"People have pretty much opened the doorway of opportunity for me all the way through life. I think you can realize that I'm not kidding when I say that behind everything I do there's somebody who offers support," Harry says, as the movie's credits move across the screen.

Harry tells the audience how, with the help of his shop teacher at the Oakland Orientation Center for the Blind, he broke away from his self-imposed exile of blindness.

"I can't imagine what would have happened if the shop teacher had decided that blind people shouldn't run the power saw because they might get cut. Or that we shouldn't water-ski because we might drown."

Harry's audience is mesmerized listening to him speak and looking at the final image on the screen: a picture of

Harry flying over the jump ramp at Cypress Gardens in Florida.

"I'm very fortunate that I've met people who have helped me achieve my goals. A lot of people think I've been dealt a pretty bad hand of cards. But it isn't the cards you're dealt, it's what you do with them and how you play them that matters.

"I thank the Lord for all the gifts I've been given. I have a lot of fun in life, and I like to think that even at the age of 55, I haven't scraped the surface yet.

"We're all so afraid of failing," Harry concludes, after reciting his signature poem, 'Keep Trying.' "Nobody wants to look inferior in front of their friends. Nobody wants to be a loser. The loser isn't the one who came in last. It's the one who never entered the race to begin with."

The lodge members stand up and give Harry hearty applause. He smiles when he hears the sound of chairs scraping the floor. He knows his message has gotten people on their feet.

When the room quiets down, he asks for questions. "And please don't raise your hands," he says. "I can't see you."

The audience laughs, and one woman comments to her husband, "I'm glad he said that. After watching him do all those things, I'd forgotten that he is blind."

A man in the back of the room calls out, "Do you develop a sixth sense that compensates for losing your sight?" It's a common question for Harry.

"Not really. Our other senses don't get any better, it's just that we make better use of them," he responds.

"Every one of you could go outside, put a blindfold on, and within minutes, you could tell which way the traffic is flowing on the street. You could tell if you were walking close to something. We learn to use our memory and our senses, because we don't have any other choice. Either we form mental images of what we're doing and where we're going, or we're lost."

The audience starts to disperse for the evening. A few people crowd around Harry, asking him questions.

"I'd like you to speak to my son's school," one woman

tells Harry. "This is just the kind of thing they need to hear."

John Butterfield is a top masters division runner, and has spent his life around civilian and military athletes. He always has been in awe of Harry's abilities, even as he egged his friend on to a sub-three-hour marathon in Boston. Athletic ability wasn't the only characteristic of Harry's to turn John into a fan. As former executive director of the President's Council on Physical Fitness and Sports, Harry's message impressed him as well.

"Harry has gotten many people who would have shriveled up and withdrawn to go out and walk and run and live," says John.

"He is a tremendous inspiration for the blind and the disabled, and for everyone else as well. He's absolutely fantastic with any audience. He has a way of gearing the presentation to any group. He has fun with children and talks to them at their level. And he endears himself to an older audience.

"He makes people feel good that they're listening to him. He has a wonderful way of encouraging people to do more with their life than they may already be doing."

Harry's accomplishments are the basis for his motivational message, but attitude also is an integral ingredient, says his sister Nancy.

"He once gave me a book about a man who was worse off than he was, and had also managed to rise above his situation. I was very depressed at the time. It was Harry's way of saying, 'Be an optimist in life. Make the most out of what you have.' He taught me to make goals for myself and to have faith that I will get there."

At the age of one and a half, Harry received his first pair of eyeglasses; spectacles so small that they had to be tied to his head with silky ribbons. That was the first of many frightening trips to the eye doctor's office, and the beginning of a journey that would lead him from the depths of depression and apathy to international recognition, a room full of athletic trophies, and letters of thanks and praise from civic leaders, school kids, and disabled colleagues.

"As I look back over the events and experiences which have made my life what it is today, I feel that I am indeed a very fortunate person.

"In 1978, my friends Joe and Carol Lewis invited me to participate in the opening ceremonies of the Special Olympics in Hawaii, the day before I tried my first 50-mile run.

"We joined the parade of athletes, and as we marched past the grandstand to the enthusiastic cheers of the crowd, I recalled what it had been like when I was in high school. Anyone with a physical handicap was automatically excused from all physical education. I had never known the meaning of sportsmanship or what it was like to compete, alone or with a team.

"Fortunately, times have changed, and I felt so lucky to be a part of that. I wasn't on the track with one handicapped person, but with hundreds of them from all over the state, and everyone could be proud of their accomplishments in the games, regardless of who won. Their performances on the field would be an education for those who watched from the stands."

Joe escorted Harry to the end of the track straightaway, where they would begin their quarter-mile demonstration loop around the stadium. The two ran in smooth tandem rhythm by the grandstand, with the announcer cataloging Harry's accomplishments over the loudspeaker. The crowd cheered, motivating Harry to do more than demonstrate technique. He cut loose and kicked up his heels to a racing pace.

"Slow down, slow down," Joe told him. "Remember you have to run 50 miles tomorrow."

Harry and Joe finished their run and headed for the field to watch the games.

"What happened next left such an impression on me," he remembers. "Many of those who had been standing on the field rushed over to me, and one by one, they put notebooks and programs into my hand and asked for my autograph. One slightly mentally handicapped child said, 'I didn't know blind people could run that fast, and you can do everything.'

"Right then, I knew for sure that I would conquer that 50-mile race if I had to crawl to the finish line."

Through the years, Harry has been a role model for people with disabilities, says Charles Buell, who met Harry during his stint as a Cal State student.

Legally blind himself, Charles was for many years the wrestling coach at the California School for the Blind in Berkeley.

"Disabled people are told over and over, 'You can't do this. You can't do that,'" says Charles, who founded the California Association of Blind Athletes in the mid-1970s. "Blind wrestlers have won championships in state meets around the country. The boys got a lot of confidence from being able to demonstrate that they could do something as well as sighted boys.

"The biggest problem we have is convincing the able-bodied that the blind have capabilities. You can do a lot more than you think you can, you just have to try. That's been Harry's philosophy all along, to encourage people to try. You'll never know until you get in there.

"Harry's made a tremendous contribution to the image of blindness. He's a missionary for blind people."

In 1992, Harry flew to Atlanta, Georgia to receive the Healthy American Fitness Leader Award, an honor given by the U.S. Chamber of Commerce to ten people a year who have made a significant contribution as a player, policy maker, or advocate in the sports world.

Harry talks about the awards ceremony with the enthusiasm of a kid on Christmas morning. He couldn't quite believe he was joining ranks with Jack LaLanne, former President Ronald Reagan, Donna DeVerona, Dorothy Hamill, and Capt. John Butterfield—all past recipients of the award.

"We stayed at the Ritz-Carlton, and Dorothy Hamill was the master of ceremonies. She gave all of us a kiss as we received our trophy. John Butterfield was one of the presenters, and Dr. Ken Cooper got it this year as well. I got to meet Arnold Palmer, who was in town for a golf tournament. He was just as nice and gracious as could be."

In 1989, Harry received the Tolland Foundation Award for Outstanding Achievement in improving the quality of life for the disabled. The award prompted an avalanche of letters recognizing Harry as a living symbol of personal achievement.

"Those two awards are unbelievable honors," says Harry. "I've been recognized for something I really believe in. My whole life is built on the confidence I've gotten through sports and athletic activities. It's really something.

"Sports turned my life around. Learning to water-ski and run and swim gave me a willingness to face challenges, despite my fears. That's something I want to share with other people. And the fact that I'm handicapped makes the message that much clearer. It motivates people to face their own limitations," says Harry.

"I have been told many times since childhood that if a person really enjoys a job, it doesn't seem like work. No matter how packed my schedule may be with training, marathons, competitions, and appearances, I enjoy every minute of it.

"Whether I'm called upon to show a few slides, lecture, or include a demonstration, I always come away at the end with a good feeling that several lives may be richer, happier, and more meaningful because people took the time to listen.

"Speaking to people is my way of saying, 'Thank you, God, for what you have given me,'" Harry says. "All you can do is the best you can. That's all. And I've had the chance to do so much.

"I don't wake up in the morning thinking, 'What would it be like to be sighted?' I don't think in those terms. I ask myself instead, 'What am I going to do today? What *can* I do?' If someone asks, 'Can you play the violin?', most people's answer right away is, 'No.' But I really believe the best attitude is: I don't know. I haven't tried yet."

KEEP TRYING

With faith that's strong, your greatest goals,
You'll conquer by and by.
Though disappointment threatens now,
Don't be afraid to try.
It really doesn't matter
If you fail or drop the ball.
The only real losers quit
Or never try at all.
So give it everything you've got,
And keep that courage high.
And if you do, you'll win the prize
That money cannot buy.
You'll always walk with honor
As there is no greater pride
Than knowing, whether win or lose,
With all your heart, you tried.

—Harry Cordellos, 1980.

*H*arry C. Cordellos is a blind athlete who lives and works in San Francisco. Determined to become the best he could be at whatever he undertook, he learned to take photographs, to run (marathons), water-ski, snow ski, hang glide, and do almost anything else he wanted to do. Harry enjoys public speaking, inspiring others to pursue their dreams and to live up to their potential. **To inquire about having Harry bring his message of inspiration to colleges, conventions, and meetings, call or write:** WRS Speakers Bureau, P.O. Box 21207, Waco, Texas 76702-1207.

*J*anet Wells is a professional writer living in Berkeley, California. She has worked as a journalist and in publishing in New York City and has traveled extensively. She is an avid outdoorswoman.

Guru's Foundation is dedicated to "feeding a civilization." Endowed by its equity ownership in Guru's restaurants, where employees are actually paid to donate time each month in community service, Guru's Foundation is building a 3500-acre retreat in Utah's High Uinta mountains. If you believe, as we do, that a life without service is a life without meaning, then we invite you to find out more about us at our Web site: www.gurusfoundation.com.

Printed in the United States
96978LV00006B/55-84/A